early years
wishing well

Collected rhymes, stories, songs and information text

People who help us

Author
Susan Gray

Editor
Clare Miller

Designer
Heather C Sanneh

Compilers
Stories, rhymes and information text compiled by Jackie Andrews

Songs compiled by Peter Morrell

Assistant Editor
Lesley Sudlow

Series Designer
Anna Oliwa

Illustrations
Louise Gardner

Cover artwork
Alex Ayliffe

Acknowledgement:
Qualifications and Curriculum Authority for the use of extracts from the QCA/DfEE document *Curriculum guidance for the foundation stage* © 2000 Qualifications and Curriculum Authority.

The publishers gratefully acknowledge permission to reproduce the following copyright material:

Jackie Andrews for the use of 'Mr Owl's helpers' and 'The park keeper's birthday' © 2002, Jackie Andrews, both previously unpublished; **Clive Barnwell** for the use of 'Friends' and 'The lorry driver' © 2002, Clive Barnwell, both previously unpublished; **Richard Caley** for the use of 'Lifeboat crew' © 2002, Richard Caley, previously unpublished; **Susan Eames** for the use of 'What is in the library?', 'Delivering the milk' and 'My gran and grandpa' © 2002, Susan Eames, all previously unpublished; **Barbara Garrad** for the use of 'Firefighters to the rescue', 'Taking care of eyes', 'The helicopter pilot' and 'Eleanor's nanny' © 2002, Barbara Garrad, all previously unpublished; **Val Jeans-Jakobsson** for the use of 'Dig, dig, dig', 'The road sweeper', 'The window cleaner' and 'A good neighbour' © 2002, Val Jeans-Jakobsson, all previously unpublished; **Karen King** for the use of 'We'll do it in no time' and 'The Clucks' car' © 2002, Karen King, both previously unpublished; **Wes Magee** for the use of 'At the vet's' and 'Dinner ladies' © 2002, Wes Magee, both previously unpublished; **Peter Morrell** for the use of 'At the baker's' and 'The shopkeeper's song' © 2002, Peter Morrell, both previously unpublished; **David Moses** for the use of 'Who took care of you?' and 'School cleaner' © 2002, David Moses, both previously unpublished; **Judith Nicholls** for the use of 'The babysitter' © 2002, Judith Nicholls, previously unpublished; **Sue Nicholls** for the use of 'Newspaper boys and girls' © 2002, Sue Nicholls, previously unpublished; **Jan Pollard** for the use of 'The busy farmer' © 2002, Jan Pollard, previously unpublished; **Hazel Priestley-Hobbs** for the use of 'Ask' and 'The school cook' © 2002, Hazel Priestley-Hobbs, both previously unpublished; **Coral Rumble** for the use of 'Up and down' 2002, Coral Rumble, previously unpublished; **Sanchia Sewell** for the use of 'My heavy bag' © 2002, Sanchia Sewell, previously unpublished; **Celia Warren** for the use of 'A policeman came to school' © 2002, Celia Warren, previously unpublished; **Kim Wilcox** for the use of 'Geraldine and the bus drivers' © 2002, Kim Wilcox, previously unpublished; **Brenda Williams** for the use of 'The hairdresser', 'Who am I?', 'The doctor' and 'The chip shop man' © 2002, Brenda Williams, all previously unpublished.

Every effort has been made to trace copyright holders and the publishers apologize for any inadvertent omissions.

Text © 2002 Susan Gray
© 2002 Scholastic Ltd

Designed using Adobe Pagemaker

Published by Scholastic Ltd, Villiers House, Clarendon Avenue, Leamington Spa, Warwickshire CV32 5PR
Visit our website at www.scholastic.co.uk
Printed by Ebenezer Baylis & Son Ltd, Worcester

1 2 3 4 5 6 7 8 9 0   2 3 4 5 6 7 8 9 0 1

British Library Cataloguing-in-Publication Data A catalogue record for this book is available from the British Library.
ISBN 0-439-01979-6

Contents

Introduction

Rhymes

Stories

Information text

Songs

Early years wishing well: People who help us

Wishing Well: People who help us

The *Wishing Well* series provides a user-friendly way for practitioners to plan for children's learning, linked to a relevant theme. There is a wealth of ideas that meet the requirements of the Early Learning Goals. The books all include rhymes, stories, information text, songs, topic ideas and photocopiable sheets.

Theme

From the moment that children are born, they come into contact with a wide variety of 'people who help them', making this a topic that every child will be able to contribute to.

Work on this theme can be made most meaningful and relevant by drawing on the children's own first-hand experiences as a starting point. The children's learning can then be extended further by the use of resources and artefacts, provided and created by both adults and children, as well as visits to the setting from relevant people and outings to places in the community.

Using an anthology

Throughout the book, you can dip into a wide range of rhymes, stories and songs that are fun to use and are appropriate for children throughout the Foundation Stage.

Information text is provided to introduce the children to facts relating to the theme and photocopiable sheets are available for a wide selection of activities.

Early Learning Goals

This book provides a wealth of resources that enable you to plan appropriate learning activities, linked directly to the six Areas of Learning in the Early Learning Goals (QCA). The ideas are equally applicable to the documents on pre-school education published for Scotland, Wales and Northern Ireland.

There are rhymes, stories, songs, information text, activity ideas and photocopiable sheets. Everything is presented in a clear and concise format so that it can be incorporated easily into your planning. The resources are easy to use and the range of suggested activities take account of different ages, abilities and experience.

Using this book

Begin planning by deciding which people the children are going to learn about and which are most relevant to the children's own experience. There are a wide variety of rhymes, stories, information text and songs to select as starting points. Make a note of the pages that you are going to use and the ideas that are most suitable, remembering to ensure a balance between all Areas of Learning.

Copies of ideas can also be given to parents and carers to inform them about the theme and encourage them to initiate discussion at home. This will extend their children's learning and encourage their children to share their knowledge. There are a variety of photocopiable sheets on pages 80 to 96. These link directly to the theme and offer an easy to prepare selection of activities.

The doctor

(Action rhyme)

Harry can't come out to play today   *(shake head)*
Harry is feeling unwell   *(look miserable)*
Harry has spots on his tummy   *(point to tummy)*
Some on his bottom as well!   *(point to bottom)*

Harry can't come out to play today   *(shake head)*
Harry is staying in bed   *(hands to side of face as though sleeping)*
Mummy has sent for the doctor   *(pretend to phone)*
And here's what the doctor said

Harry must take some medicine   *(mime pouring medicine into spoon and swallowing)*
Harry will soon feel okay   *(smile)*
Harry can play out tomorrow
But Harry can't play out today.   *(shake head)*

> *Mime as suggested or role-play.*

Brenda Williams

The doctor

Personal, social and emotional development

★ Talk about occasions when the children have visited a doctor or stayed in a hospital.

★ Discuss the feelings experienced by the children when they are ill. How do they feel if a friend or family member is sick?

★ Create a role-play doctor's surgery with the children.

Communication, language and literacy

★ As you read the rhyme, ask different children to play the various parts mentioned, as all the children join in with the actions.

★ Make 'Get Well' cards for sick people that the children know or a poorly doll or teddy in your setting.

★ On a computer, print out sheets of times throughout your day at five minute intervals. Place in a ring-binder and give the children the folder to use to make lists of appointments. Include appointment cards to give out. Use as part of the role-play for Personal, social and emotional development development (see above).

Mathematical development

★ Make some sad face pictures and count them out daily to show how many children may be at home ill.

★ Talk about how appointments at the doctors only last for a limited time. Let the children use a sand timer in the role-play area to make sure that everyone has the same length of time with the doctor.

★ Use forehead thermometers to take each other's temperature. Ask each child to write down their temperature, then sort themselves into groups with the same temperature.

Knowledge and understanding of the world

★ Show the children a stethoscope and explain why a doctor uses one. Give the children the opportunity to use one to listen to each other's hearts.

★ Talk with the children about the importance of not touching or taking medicines or tablets without an adult present.

Physical development

★ Let the children wrap short lengths of bandages around dolls and each other.

★ Borrow a pair of crutches or a wheelchair and let the children see how this changes the way that they move and where they can go.

Creative development

★ Create a 'Miss Polly' dolly with either plasters or red spots stuck on and bandages. Sing the song in *This Little Puffin…* compiled by Elizabeth Matterson (Puffin) and take it in turns to comfort the doll by rocking her.

★ Make spotty masks from paper plates. Paint sad faces on each plate and glue on circles of red paper. Cut out eye-holes for the children and attach elastic across the back.

At the vet's

We sit and wait
    to see the vet.
We're here with Rusty,
    Gran's sick pet.

She's a kitten
    Gran took in.
A starving stray
    so weak, and thin.

Gran found Rusty
    at her door,
with bitten ear
    and poorly paw.

In her basket
    Rusty cries
and looks at me
    with sad round eyes.

We wait with Rusty,
    Gran's sick pet.
We sit and wait
    to see the vet.

Wes Magee

Early years wishing well: People who help us

At the vet's

Personal, social and emotional development

★ During circle time, give the children the opportunity to talk about their pets and taking care of them.

★ Discuss with the children how an animal might feel at the vet's.

★ Encourage the children to talk about how we feel when a pet is ill or dies.

★ Create a role-play vet's surgery with the children using toy animals that they can bring from home.

Communication, language and literacy.

★ Give each child a copy of the photocopiable sheet on page 80. Ask them to trace over the letters, then match the pet to the word.

★ Make shopping lists of things to buy to take care of and feed a new pet. Encourage the children to begin each list with a picture of their chosen animal.

★ Create a group book of the children's pets, using photographs or drawings. Label the types of pet and talk about the book together.

★ Invite the children to make a list of their pet's names.

★ Create a display of animal books and stories.

Mathematical development

★ Make a graph of the children's pets, or favourite pets of those that do not have one.

★ Sort pictures of pets into sets such as 'How many legs?'.

★ Look at pictures of different pet animals and put them in size order.

Knowledge and understanding of the world

★ Invite someone to visit with a pet animal, if possible one that has been rescued or has been to see a vet.

★ Observe minibeasts in your outdoor environment. Give the children the opportunity to take photographs and use magnifying glasses and binoculars.

Physical development

★ Encourage the children to think about how they could move like an animal, for example, trot like a horse, swim like a fish or hop like a rabbit.

★ Ask individual children to mime an animal for the others to guess.

★ Provide small lengths of bandage for the children to put carefully on toy pets.

Creative development

★ Paint pictures of poorly pets. Display them in a line waiting to see the vet.

★ Make pets in carrying boxes. Make two holes in the lid of a shoebox. Thread through ribbon or string to create a handle. Glue the lid on to the box and ask the children to draw the face of their pet, cut it out and stick it on to the front of the box.

Early years wishing well: People who help us

Up and down

The dentist's chair goes up and up,
He lets me have a ride,
And then he tells me to lie back
And open my mouth wide.

He looks inside my wide, wide mouth
To check my teeth are white,
To check that they won't hurt me when
I chew my food or bite.

The dentist's chair goes down and down,
He smiles and gives a wave,
And when I leave I get a badge
To show that I've been brave.

Coral Rumble

Early years wishing well: People who help us

Up and down

Personal, social and emotional development

★ Discuss with the children their own experiences of visiting the dentist and caring for teeth. Talk about why it is important to look after our teeth and what everyone can do to keep their teeth healthy.

★ Provide unbreakable mirrors for the children to use to look at their own teeth.

Communication, language and literacy

★ Act as a scribe to write out the rhyming words in the poem: ride/wide, white/bite and wave/brave. Invite the children to suggest other rhyming words.

★ Collect a variety of toothpaste boxes and see how many times you can find the word 'toothpaste' on the boxes. Ask the children to help you look.

★ Write out words beginning with 't' such as teeth, toothpaste, tongue and toothbrush. Use the words to label a picture or items on a 'touch and talk' display.

Mathematical development

★ Create a recording chart for each child to take home for seven days. Tell parents and carers that you have been talking about keeping teeth healthy and ask them to help their child to fill in the chart with a tick each time they have cleaned their teeth; one tick after breakfast and another before bed each day. If any of the children forget, ask them to

draw a cross on the chart. Ask them to return their charts and count out how many times they have brushed their teeth in a week and how many times they forgot.

Knowledge and understanding of the world

★ Invite parents and carers to bring babies along to the setting to show the children what babies eat. Look at the different foods and discuss with the children how the food changes as a baby becomes older and has teeth.

★ Look at animal books to find pictures of animal teeth, especially those belonging to big meat-eating animals such as crocodiles or dinosaurs.

Physical development

★ Ask the children to bring in their toothbrushes and toothpaste in a named bag. As a whole group, talk about the correct way to clean teeth. In small groups, practise brushing teeth.

Creative development

★ Create a display of food pictures in two sections, showing those that are good and those that are bad for our teeth. Provide the children with a selection of food shapes cut out from appropriately-coloured sheets of paper. Use toothbrushes to brush paint across the paper or flick the bristles to splatter paint onto the paper.

Who am I?

I am a special person
A person that you know
I'm always there to meet you
In rain or sun or snow.

I stand on zebra crossings
And make the traffic stop
I wear a special shiny coat
And wave a lollipop!

Brenda Williams

Early years wishing well: People who help us

Who am I?

Personal, social and emotional development

★ In an outdoor play area or large space, mark the ground with chalk to create a pretend road and zebra crossing. Provide a selection of dressing-up clothes so that the children can either dress as pedestrians or as crossing patrol people. Intervene at appropriate times to ask the children to cross you over their road safely.

★ Discuss the importance of road safety and always crossing the road with an adult.

Communication, language and literacy

★ Show the children a crossing patrol person's lollipop (or a picture of one) and talk about why the word 'Stop' is written on it and who needs to stop.

★ Give each child a copy of the photocopiable sheet on page 81 copied on to card. Ask them to follow the dotted lines to complete the picture. Cut out the pictures and use for role-play.

Mathematical development

★ Arrange a selection of wooden 3-D shapes and ask the children if they can find any which are the same shapes as ice-creams or lollipops.

★ Give the children a large packet of wrapped fruit lollipops. Invite the children to look at them and, without counting, guess which flavour there are the most and least of.

Sort the lollies into sets of each flavour. Ask the children to count out which flavour there are the most and least of and see if their guesses were correct.

Knowledge and understanding of the world

★ Visit real zebra and pelican crossings near your setting and show the children how they should be used with an adult.

★ Make or buy ice lollies and enjoy eating them. (Check for allergies and dietary requirements.) Ask the children to observe their lolly melting as they begin to eat it.

★ Add frozen lollies to water in the water tray and observe them as they melt and change the colour of the water.

Physical development

★ Make crossing patrol persons' 'lollipops' from broom handles with thick card circles attached to each one. Encourage the children to use these safely during play sessions to stop other children riding in cars and on bikes.

★ Play musical statues and encourage all the children to stop quickly, without touching anyone else.

Creative development

★ Paint old cereal boxes to make lollipops and attach kitchen-roll tubes as sticks.

★ Look at photographs of zebras. Draw pictures of zebras on grey sugar paper using black and white pastel crayons.

Dinner ladies

I spoon up
all the gravy,
sausage-pie,
and peas,
and the dinner ladies
say to me,

'Mind your manners, please!'

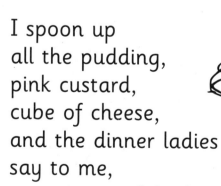

I spoon up
all the pudding,
pink custard,
cube of cheese,
and the dinner ladies
say to me,

'Mind your manners, please!'

Wes Magee

Dinner ladies

Personal, social and emotional development

★ Create a café or dining area with an assortment of play food, knives, forks and spoons. If possible, include other resources such as chopsticks and stainless steel cups and bowls.

★ Visit a school's kitchen and ask a dinner lady to talk to the children and show them around the kitchen.

★ Discuss table manners and why they are important.

Communication, language and literacy

★ Provide A4 sheets of card for the children to create menus on. Ask them to include drawings of food to illustrate their menu.

★ Make a collection of simple recipe books for your book area.

★ Cut up a selection of fruit such as bananas, strawberries and oranges. Write the names of the fruits on matching coloured card, for example, bananas on yellow card, strawberries on red card and so on. Invite the children to smell each fruit and guess what they are. Hold up the correct card when a child guesses correctly.

Mathematical development

★ Give the children the opportunity to pay for food items in a role-play café.

★ Make a set of 'shadow mats' for the home area, showing the shapes and colours of cutlery and crockery, so that the children can set each place accurately.

Knowledge and understanding of the world

★ Make jellies in a selection of moulds. When set, turn out and hold a 'jelly tea party'.

★ Talk about the importance of washing hands and drying them properly before a meal and practise doing this daily.

★ Show the children a shopping bag filled with fruit and vegetables and take items out one by one. Encourage the children to name each item and guess if the food is grown in this country or not. Ask the children to guess which items grow in hot places.

Physical development

★ Give the children a variety of moulds to create shapes of food in wet sand.

★ Let the children spread jam on biscuits or toast for snack time.

Creative development

★ Make 'favourite dinners' plates of food. Give each child a paper plate and a selection of different-coloured tissue paper to scrunch together, cut out, tear and glue to create food to stick on their plate.

★ Give each child a copy of the photocopiable sheet on page 82. Ask them to draw their favourite dinners on the plate.

★ Make prints using real fruit and vegetables cut in half.

The window cleaner

(Action rhyme)

Up the ladder and start to clean
The dirtiest window you've ever seen!

Wash and wipe and rub again
Clean away at the window pane.

Polish it dry until there's a shine
The dust has gone and so has the grime.

Back down the ladder and start again,
Plenty to do – BUT it's started to rain!

> *Actions: 'climbing' up and down ladder, and cleaning movements.*

Val Jeans-Jakobsson

Early years wishing well: People who help us

The window cleaner

Personal, social and emotional development

★ Place a box of spring-cleaning items in your home area including dusters, cloths, mops, brushes and buckets to encourage the children to play at keeping their home clean.

Communication, language and literacy

★ Discuss the concept of upstairs and downstairs. Encourage the children to discuss their own home and talk about whether they live on one level or more.
★ Ask the children to draw pictures and write down the names of rooms in their home.

Mathematical development

★ Collect estate agent's details of houses and count the windows at the front of each house. Discuss the shapes of the windows and see how many shapes you can find.
★ Draw a simple sheet of window shapes and let the children take it home with a letter for parents and carers asking them to help their child to count how many windows of each shape are at the front of their home and to record the numbers next to the relevant shapes. Use the findings to identify which shapes of window are the most common.

Knowledge and understanding of the world

★ Go on a local walk to observe as many types of window as you can. Compare the differences between windows on old and new buildings.
★ Visit a local church or special building to look at very large windows and, if possible, stained-glass windows.
★ Give the children the opportunity to blow bubbles outdoors and observe the different sizes and colours on the surface.

Physical development

★ Put a selection of sponges and cloths in the water tray. Encourage the children to wet them and try squeezing them out until they are almost dry.
★ Ask the children to mime wiping windows with a cloth and pretend to climb up and down a ladder. Encourage them to reach up high and down low to ensure that all of the windows are clean.

Creative development

★ Cut house shapes out of large sheets of paper and provide the children with sponges to print windows and doors using square and rectangle shapes.
★ Ask the children to paint pictures of the view from their bedroom window. When they are dry, stick on cut-up fabric pieces to represent curtains.
★ Make a stained-glass window by sticking a collage of different-coloured pieces of tissue on a plastic surface with PVA glue. When it is completely dry, peel it off in one sheet and fix to a window.

What is in the library?

What is in the library?
Would you like a book?
Stories, facts and poems,
everywhere you look.
What is in the library?
A box of cuddly toys.
Would you like to read to one?
They're here for girls and boys.
What is in the library?
A copying machine.
Video tapes of cartoon films
You've probably never seen.
Tapes of all your favourite books,
stories you will know.
Posters of events in town.
Perhaps you'd like to go?
What's happening in the library?
A Story Time in June.
You can come to Story Time –
There's going to be one soon.
Who is in the library?
Grown-ups, children, too,
Bringing back the things they borrowed,
choosing something new.

Susan Eames

Early years wishing well: People who help us

What is in the library?

Personal, social and emotional development

★ Set up a library role-play area, containing a selection of books for adults, children and babies. Ask the children to sort the books into different sections by themselves. The children can then choose which age group they belong to when they play in the library.

★ During circle time, discuss the meaning of lending and borrowing things and why it is important to look after things and return them safely. Talk about how the children feel if they want something that does not belong to them and discuss sharing resources with others in your setting.

Communication, language and literacy

★ Make story tapes of familiar stories and introduce a tape of a new story after reading it. More able children may enjoy recording a story with you to share with their friends.

★ Make a large class book about nursery rhymes. Include illustrations by the children and write each rhyme out on the computer with each child. Read a selection of rhymes daily and display the book in the book area for the children to use independently.

★ Set up your own library system and give the children the opportunity to borrow a book each week.

Mathematical development

★ Count out four sets of five books with a group of children. Make sets by using books from the same series in each set so that they look similar. Take away one or more book from three of the sets and see if the children can work out how many are missing. As the children become more able, make sets of another number.

Knowledge and understanding of the world

★ Observe at a map of your local area and discuss where the nearest library is. If possible, arrange to go on a visit or arrange a book bus to visit you.

★ Look at a range of books from various cultures and discuss the different writing.

Physical development

★ Talk about the importance of handling books with care and using them the correct way up. Support children who find it difficult to look at a book correctly and share turning the pages.

Creative development

★ Paint pictures to illustrate book covers of well-known teddy bear characters. See how many different ones the children can think of. Display these with a collection of teddies.

★ Make a music tape or CD area so that the children can listen to music and join in singing. Invite one child each day to bring a favourite song from home to share with the rest of the group.

Delivering the milk

(Action rhyme)

Driving to the dairy,
Early in the morning,
Driving to the dairy
When we're still asleep.

(hands on the steering wheel)

Loading up the crates,
Early in the morning,
Loading up the crates
When we're still asleep.

(lift the crates)

Driving down the street,
Early in the morning,
Driving down the street
When we're still asleep.

(driving again)

Putting bottles on the doorstep,
Early in the morning,
Putting bottles on the doorstep
When we're still asleep.

(bend down with the bottles)

Taking back the empties,
Early in the morning,
Taking back the empties
When we're still asleep.

(pick up the empties and drive back to the dairy)

Susan Eames

Delivering the milk

Personal, social and emotional development

★ Talk with the children about whether they have milk delivered at home. Discuss who likes milk, who dislikes it and talk about allergies.

★ If you have drinks time, take it in turns for each child to give out straws and encourage all the children to handle bottles and cups carefully.

Communication, language and literacy

★ Read the story of 'Goldilocks and the Three Bears'. Ask the children if they think the bears had their milk delivered for their breakfast or if they visited a shop.

Mathematical development

★ Display a milk crate containing four or six bottles of milk. Each day, change the amount of bottles in the crate that are full and empty and count them as a group.

★ Have a daily delivery of clean plastic milk containers in the home corner. At home time, put out a note to show how many are needed tomorrow. Make mistakes sometimes so that the children can tell you how many are missing or how many extras have been delivered.

★ Give each child a copy of the photocopiable sheet on page 83. Ask them to colour their house. As a group, number each door to create a house number line.

Knowledge and understanding of the world

★ Talk to the children about where milk comes from and what other dairy products are produced.

★ Make porridge using milk and have a 'Three Bears' breakfast. Be aware of any children who may have allergies.

★ Ask the children to think about where dairy products are stored both in shops and at their home. Discuss the reasons why these things need to be kept cold.

Physical development

★ Fill large, plastic fizzy drink bottles with a small amount of sand and arrange them like a set of skittles. Give the children a few balls to roll at the bottles and see who can knock down the most. Use different-sized balls to change the level of difficulty.

★ Practise pouring water from jugs into plastic cups without spilling any.

Creative development

★ Fill ten glass bottles with different quantities of water and arrange them in a line. Give the children a wooden beater and encourage them to listen to the range of sounds they can make.

★ Sing 'Ten milk bottles sitting on the wall' to the tune of 'Ten Green Bottles'.

★ Make observational drawings of bottles. Offer a range of shapes and colours so that the children can choose their own.

The road sweeper

The road sweeper is coming
With his brush and cart.
There's so much litter lying about
He won't know where to start!

Don't drop your rubbish on the floor,
Don't leave it lying around.
Just put it in the litter bin
Not scattered on the ground.

Next time you have a wrapper
– a chocolate bar or sweet
or empty packet from your crisps,
don't drop it by your feet.

The road sweeper has finished
This place looks clean and neat
Let's try to keep it tidy!
Who wants a messy street?

Val Jeans-Jakobsson

Early years wishing well: People who help us

The road sweeper

Personal, social and emotional development

★ Create road sweepers by attaching small brushes to prams or pushchairs, so that the children can play at road sweeping.

★ Discuss the importance of using litter bins to dispose of rubbish. Ask the children to identify bins around the room and if applicable outside, to help them become more aware of them. Remind the children that litter can be dirty and never to take things out of bins.

Communication, language and literacy

★ Cut out letters in a variety of textures including sandpaper, wallpaper, sugar paper, card and metallic paper. Encourage the children to trace over the letters and describe the feeling of each surface.

★ Act as a scribe to write down words that the children suggest, beginning with the letter 's'. Use individual whiteboards and pens to encourage the children to write some of the words or letters. Invite the children to bring a named item beginning with 's' from home and create a display of them all.

Mathematical development

★ Talk about collecting up leaves when they fall. Collect some autumn leaves and order them according to size starting with the shortest.

★ Cut sponges into rectangle shapes of various sizes and print with them, starting with the smallest.

Knowledge and understanding of the world

★ Create an autumn area for the children to bring their own collections of autumn things that they have found on the ground. Display non-fiction books about autumn and the other seasons.

★ Discuss why a type of salt is put on to road surfaces during icy weather. Give the children plastic beakers and let them stir in table salt with teaspoons and watch it dissolve.

★ Go on a 'puddle walk' after a recent rainfall to discover puddles around your setting. Ask the children to consider why puddles are in some places and not in others.

Physical development

★ Encourage the children to put on and take off wellington boots by themselves. Ask them to keep their boots together using clothes pegs.

★ Let the children use different types of brushes to sweep up fallen leaves.

Creative development

★ Use small paint rollers to make roadway pictures. Make lines in yellow and white paint on large sheets of black sugar paper. Cut the sugar paper into curved and straight shapes.

★ Make leaf prints in autumn colours and stick them on to red paper.

A policeman came to school

A policeman came to school today.
This is what he had to say:

Keep away from railways,
Don't play on the road,
Never talk to strangers
Or people you don't know.

Take a good friend with you
if you're playing in the park.
Tell Mum where you're going
and be home before it's dark.

That's what the policeman had to say
When he came to school today.

Celia Warren

Early years wishing well: People who help us

A policeman came to school

Personal, social and emotional development

★ Invite a policeman or policewoman to visit your setting and talk to the children about their job. If this is not possible, discuss their role as a whole group. Talk about what the police do to help people.

★ Discuss nearby rail tracks and ask the children to think of the dangers regarding playing near to them.

Communication, language and literacy

★ Play 'Kim's Game' by placing several toy emergency vehicles on a tray and naming each one with the children. Cover over the vehicles with a tea towel and remove one without the children seeing. Can the children name the missing vehicle?

★ Provide the children with small notebooks to make statements, descriptions of criminals and details of imaginary crimes.

Mathematical development

★ Make a copy for each child of the dot-to-dot on the photocopiable sheet on page 84 and ask them to join the dots.

★ Sort a collection of silver and gold buttons into sets, for example, silver and gold, ones with and without designs on, round and other shapes and the number of holes.

★ Play 'How many are missing?' by asking the children to count how many pieces are missing from familiar jigsaws. Place the missing pieces around the room and the children play detectives to find them. As each piece is found, they can count up again how many are left to find.

★ Encourage the children to find missing items at tidy-up time.

Knowledge and understanding of the world

★ Provide a selection of hand magnifying glasses and encourage the children to look at their fingers and see the pattern of their fingerprints. Using washable ink-pads, the children can print their set onto paper and view each other's fingerprints.

★ Look at books about people who help us and notice the range of different uniforms.

Physical development

★ Give the children the opportunity to fasten buttons and dress up in role-play uniforms.

★ Make puppets in uniform using the puppet templates on the photocopiable sheets on pages 85 and 86. Copy on to card, colour, decorate and cut out the individual puppets. Write each title on a lolly stick and mount the puppets on to them.

Creative development

★ Create fingerprint paintings of ladybirds by printing spots and eyes using black paint onto cut-out red ladybird shapes.

★ Paint or collage pictures of policemen and policewomen for a wall display.

Lifeboat crew

The lifeboat crew waits for a flare
Then goes to work as people stare
Stormy seas they often brave
Plucking sailors from the waves.

Richard Caley

Early years wishing well: People who help us

Lifeboat crew

Personal, social and emotional development

★ Create boats on the sea using empty paddling pools or baby baths with blown-up swimming rings by the sides. Ask the children to imagine being aboard a sinking ship, rescuing people, or being rescued.

★ During circle time, talk about safety on boats and invite the children to share their experiences of boats.

★ Give the children a box of armbands, rubber rings and, if possible, a life jacket. Encourage them to put the items on by themselves.

Communication, language and literacy

★ Photocopy and enlarge the poem or write it out big for a large group to see clearly and read the poem as a group. Ask the children to identify the rhyming words and invite individual children to underline them. Give the children the opportunity to write down all the pairs of rhyming words that they can think of.

★ Say the rhyme 'The Owl and the Pussycat' by Edward Lear, see *Bisky Bats and Pussy Cats* (Bloomsbury) and pick out examples of rhyming words.

★ Make wavy-pattern tracing cards for the children to trace over.

Mathematical development

★ Collect wine bottle corks and float them in water. Give the children plastic containers with numbers on them (you could use a marker pen or nail varnish). Ask the children to fill the containers with the correct number of corks by scooping them out of the water.

Knowledge and understanding of the world

★ Look at a globe and discuss which parts are land and which are sea.

★ Make boats out of foil or Plasticine. See if the boats can be loaded with small plastic beads or bricks.

★ Ask the children to bring in items that float from home and test them in the water tray. Provide a selection of objects that sink so they can be tested, too.

Physical development

★ Practise a rowing action using plastic oars and an inflatable dingy.

★ Sit in a large circle and role-play rowing boats across a river from one side to the other. Row quickly when the crocodile comes along!

Creative development

★ Paint lines in a range of shades of blue across sheets of white paper. When this background is dry, cut out two large triangles and a rectangle in black paper and stick on to make a yacht on the sea.

★ Make wave pictures by combing through thick paint using large combs. Add a little sand to create a beach effect.

Dig, dig, dig

First we must start to use the spade.
Dig – dig – dig.
Clear the weeds and a space is made.
Dig – dig – dig.

Rake the earth until it is fine.
Rake – rake – rake.
Smooth it out in a good straight line.
Rake – rake – rake.

Next we'll put the seeds in the ground.
Plant – plant – plant.
Cover with earth – leave a space around.
Plant – plant – plant.

Time goes by and the plants have grown.
Pick – pick – pick.
Vegetables grew from the seeds we've sown.
Pick – pick – pick.

Back to the kitchen now, ready to clean.
Wash – wash – wash.
Cabbages, carrots, onions and beans.
Wash – wash – wash.

Val Jeans-Jakobsson

Early years wishing well: People who help us

Dig, dig, dig

Personal, social and emotional development

★ Create a role-play garden centre and include a greenhouse made from a large cardboard box with a few windows cut out. Use artificial flowers and plants and a selection of children's garden tools.
★ Talk to the children about things that may grow in their gardens or nearby. Invite the children to bring in things that they or any members of their family may have grown such as flowers, runner beans or tomatoes.

Communication, language and literacy

★ Make plant labels for indoor or outdoor plants. Use real plant labels or write on clean lollipop sticks. Ask the children to place the labels in the compost or on the ground.
★ Make packets of seeds with plain white paper bags which the children can illustrate and write on. Put rice or lentils in the finished packets and seal the top so that the packets rattle like a real packet of seeds.
★ Create a 'Jack and the Beanstalk' story bag. First, read *Jack and the Beanstalk* (*Favourite Tales* series, Ladybird) and put it into a bag in your book area for the children to share. Revisit the bag together each day and add an item to the bag that links to the story, for example, a packet of bean seeds, toy hen, plastic golden egg and so on. Encourage the children to look at the book and think about the story.

Mathematical development

★ Bring in some flowers and count the petals and leaves. Some flowers may have more petals than the children can count, so encourage them to guess which has the most.
★ Collect acorns, conkers and other seeds to sort into sets and compare for size and shape.

Knowledge and understanding of the world

★ Use magnifying glasses to observe real seeds.
★ Grow bean seeds in clear glass jars filled with cotton wool soaked in water. Water these seeds each day and when large enough the children can take them home to plant.

Physical development

★ Fill an empty sand tray with compost, trowels, forks and plant pots. The children can fill the pots and handle a range of seeds.
★ If you have access to a garden, give the children the opportunity to use small spades to dig the soil.
★ Give each child a copy of the photocopiable sheet on page 87. Ask them to use sharp pencils to fill in what is missing from the items on the right of the page.

Creative development

★ Draw circles on to different-coloured paper. Let the children cut the circles out and stick them on to lolly sticks or straws to create simple flowers.

29

The busy farmer

Farmer, farmer,
Milk the cow.
Cream and butter,
We'll have now.
Farmer, farmer,
Feed the pig.
Oink, oink, oink
He's getting big.
Farmer, farmer,
Shear the sheep.
Nice warm clothes
For us to keep.
Farmer, farmer,
Cut the wheat.
Made into bread
It's good to eat.
Farmer, farmer,
Eggs for tea!
Laid by hens
For you and me.

Jan Pollard

Early years wishing well: People who help us

The busy farmer

Personal, social and emotional development

★ Set up a small-world farm, including cardboard boxes for the children to make their own buildings for vehicles and animals.

★ Collect harvest food and donate it to local retirement homes or raffle the food for charity, for example, one that helps people in other countries who may have little food, or one that helps homeless people.

Communication, language and literacy

★ Make 'parent and baby animal boxes' by placing toy farm animals in boxes such as shoeboxes. Open the 'baby boxes' one at a time and see if the children can name the animals. Ask the children to name the babies' parents and find the boxes that they are in. Write the animals' names on to cards and put them in the appropriate boxes. Place the boxes in a writing area for the children to try to read and write the words independently.

Mathematical development

★ Ask the children to count out a given number of small-world animals and put them in a specific place on the farm (see Personal, social and emotional development above), for example, 'Put five cows in the field', 'Put three lambs and one sheep in the barn' and so on. Think of as many different combinations as you can and encourage the children to ask each other to find animals.

★ As a whole group sing 'Old Macdonald Had a Farm' and create a line of toy farm animals by adding an animal to represent each verse. At the end of the song, count up the animals to see how many types Old Macdonald had. Let the children play this in small groups and give them the opportunity to count out different amounts of animals to either lengthen or shorten the song.

Knowledge and understanding of the world

★ Collect some untreated sheep's wool and sterilize it. Ask the children to feel it, describe it, and look at it using a magnifying glass. Make a collection of things made from wool and ask the children to bring items to add to a 'touch and talk' display.

★ Make bread rolls and give one to each child to take home.

Physical development

★ Make farm animals out of play dough or Plasticine.

★ Let the children carefully handle real farm produce such as eggs, strawberries and apples.

Creative development

★ Ask the children to create prints wearing old pairs of wellies by stepping into a tray of paint and walking along long sheets of paper. Hold each child's hand to ensure that they do not slip on the paint.

The chip shop man

Chip, chop, chip
the chips

Drop them in fat
and lick your lips

Cover the fish
with flour and batter

Splash them in oil
with such a splatter

Watch them cook
to a golden glow

Sieve them out
and put on show

Salt and vinegar
Wrap them well

Such a warm
and tasty smell

The chip shop man
Makes chips just right

And we buy some
Every Friday night!

Mime appropriate actions.

Brenda Williams

Early years wishing well: People who help us

The chip shop man

Personal, social and emotional development

★ Make salt-dough fish and chips with the children. Bake these until hard and set up a chip shop together. Provide aprons, and trowels or small spades to scoop up the chips and encourage the children to share them out together.

★ During circle time, ask the children if they have visited a chip shop and talk about their favourite types of food.

Communication, language and literacy

★ Write and draw warning signs on bright paper to place next to all the plug sockets around the room.

★ Make a 'Lotto' game with pictures and words of things that you could buy from the chip shop.

★ Play 'Find the fish' by showing the children a soft toy fish or a fish cut out of card. Let the children take it in turns to look away while you hide the fish. Encourage the rest of the children to give clues to help them to find it.

Mathematical development

★ Sing the song 'One, Two, Three, Four, Five' from *This Little Puffin…* compiled by Elizabeth Matterson (Puffin). Ensure that the children are holding up the correct amount of fingers as they sing the song.

★ Make a fish tank number line. Cut out ten fish and number each one. Fix a long blue rectangle onto a display board and attach the fish in the correct order with drawing pins. Each day, swap two of the fish and ask the children to tell you which ones are in the wrong order.

Knowledge and understanding of the world

★ Soak dried peas overnight to make mushy peas for the children to eat. (Check for food allergies and dietary requirements.)

★ Discuss safety in the kitchen and ask the children to suggest ways of avoiding accidents near hot things. Fold a sheet of paper into quarters and ask the children to draw four pictures of things in the kitchen that are dangerous.

★ Observe real fish in tanks and note differences and similarities.

Physical development

★ Give the children pieces of paper to wrap up the play food fish and chips.

★ Encourage the children to balance a small potato on a wooden spoon. When the children have had some practice, hold a potato and spoon race.

Creative development

★ Add salt to a range of brightly-coloured paint to create texture when dry. Ask the children to paint bright rainbow fish.

★ Make potato prints to create birthday or Christmas wrapping paper.

The hairdresser

(Action rhyme)

Snip Snip   (make scissor movement with fingers)
Snippety snip

Cutting my hair   (make scissor movement to hair)
With a clippety clip

In the mirror   (point forwards)
I can see

Judy the hairdresser   (point to own smiling face)
Smiling at me

Falling, falling   (flutter fingers downward towards the floor)
To the floor

One two three curls   (put up one, two and then three fingers)
Then some more   (extend all fingers)

In my chair   (turn around full circle)
She swirls me round

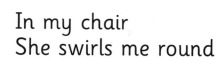

Then lowers me gently   (gradually drop to sitting on the floor)
To the ground

Brenda Williams

Early years wishing well: People who help us

The hairdresser

Personal, social and emotional development

★ Discuss with the children all the different colours and types of hair that they can think of. Ask them if their hair is similar to that of other family members or friends and discuss personal preferences.

★ Talk about who cuts the children's hair and if they enjoy having it done or not.

Communication, language and literacy

★ Ask the children to think about the stages of washing and drying their hair. Act as a scribe to write down words that they suggest and draw simple pictures. Next, ask the children to discuss the correct sequence of the actions and then let them create their own series of instructions using pictures. More able children could add words as well.

★ Tell the story of *Rapunzel* (*Favourite Tales* series, Ladybird) using a doll with a long plait of wool attached to create her long hair. Ask the children if they think it would hurt Rapunzel if someone climbed up her hair.

Mathematical development

★ Ask the children to draw a picture of their face and hair on the same-sized pieces of paper. Make a graph with the pictures to see which colours are the most and least popular.

★ Sort a tray of hair slides and bobbles into matching pairs and let the children put them on each other or on dolls.

★ Invite the children to look at everyone in the group and discuss who has the longest and shortest hair.

Knowledge and understanding of the world

★ Make 'Haircut Humptys' out of empty eggshells with faces drawn on. Fill with wet cotton wool and sprinkle a few cress seeds on the top. When his hair has grown long enough, each child can use scissors to cut the hair of their own Humpty. Make sandwiches using the cress for a picnic together.

★ Look at pictures and photographs of hair styles from long ago and discuss how they may look different from those today.

★ Ask the children to bring in photographs of themselves as babies and talk about how their hair has changed over time.

★ Discuss why people from some religions or cultures do not cut their hair.

Physical development

★ Put dried spaghetti into an empty water tray and let the children practise cutting it up, pretending that it is very long hair.

★ Give each child a copy of the photocopiable sheeet on page 88. Invite them to cut up pieces of wool and stick them on the sheet to make hairstyles of their choice.

Creative development

★ Create a lion picture using curly wood shavings to create his mane.

The babysitter

What we said

Can we stay up late?
Mum *always* lets us
stay till 8!

Can we watch TV?
Please, this is one
we *always* see!

Can we have some bread?
We *always* eat
before we go to bed!

Can we stay and play?
We *always* stay up late
when Mum's away...

What the babysitter said

No play,
  no bread,
   no TV,
    just

BED!

NOW!

Judith Nicholls

Early years wishing well: People who help us

The babysitter

Personal, social and emotional development

★ Give the children the opportunity to be babysitters themselves by taking it in turns to take 'Bedtime Bear' home. Put a teddy in a bag with a bedtime story-book and his own blanket or sleeping bag. Discuss with the children how they feel when someone takes care of them and ask them to think of ways that they could make Teddy feel safe.

★ Talk about who babysits for the children.

Communication, language and literacy

★ Put a diary in 'Bedtime Bear's' bag for parents and carers to write in about what he did and where he went when he came to stay. Share the stories from his diary at the start of each day.

Mathematical development

★ Make clock-faces from card and attach hands using split pins. Send a note to parents and carers asking them to write down the time that their children go to bed. Help the children to move the hands of their clock to display their bedtime.

★ Collect ten teddies or dolls and line them up in a cot or large box with a cover on. Sing 'There Were Ten in a Bed' from *This Little Puffin…* compiled by Elizabeth Matterson (Puffin). Ask the children to take out the toys one by one and count up each time how many are left.

Knowledge and understanding of the world

★ Discuss animals that come out at night and make a display of books about nocturnal animals.

★ Set up a small tent indoors and let the children use torches inside to pretend that they are camping. Ask them to consider the reasons why they would need a torch and discuss sources of light in the home.

Physical development

★ Encourage the children to put pillows into pillow cases for the home area.

★ In a large open space, encourage the children to mime getting undressed, putting on pyjamas ready for bed, brushing teeth, lying down ready to go to sleep and eventually falling asleep. Ask the children to wake up after their sleep and stretch out their bodies as much as they can.

Creative development

★ Make a 'Ten in the bed' wall collage by drawing around ten children, from the waist upwards, and using a variety of collage materials to decorate their bodies and to make a large quilt to cover them.

★ Make bedtime pictures using one circle and two rectangles of paper, one a little smaller than the other. Paint patterns on the smallest rectangle, for the quilt and a face on the circle and stick onto the largest rectangle to represent the bed.

A good neighbour

Some people said that Mrs B was the most helpful person in the village. If anyone asked her to do something for them, she would always say, 'Yes, of course!'

One morning, she was setting off to go shopping in town, when her neighbour called out, 'Oh, Mrs B, could you please get me some carrots while you're in town?'

'Yes, of course!' said Mrs B, and she walked on down the hill.

'Oh, Mrs B!' called her friend from across the street. 'Could you please get me a box of six eggs?'

'Yes, of course!' said Mrs B, and she crossed the road to the bus stop.

Mrs B hopped on the bus when it came, and went into town.

When she had done all her shopping, Mrs B returned home. She took the carrots and eggs to her neighbours, then she went indoors and made herself a cup of tea.

Later that day, there came a ring at the doorbell. It was the neighbour who asked her to buy some carrots. She was carrying a little bowl with cling film on the top, and a delicious smell was coming from it.

'I made some chicken stew with those carrots you bought for me, and I thought you might like some for your supper,' she said.

Mrs B was delighted. 'Oh, how lovely. Now I shan't need to cook tonight!'

A little later there was another ring at the doorbell. It was the friend who asked her to get the eggs.

'I made some cakes with those eggs you bought for me, and I thought you might like these.' She held out a plate with four little cakes on it. Each had white icing and a cherry on top.

Mrs B was delighted. 'Oh, how lovely. Now I shan't need to do any baking! Thank you!'

'Not at all,' said her friend. 'One good turn deserves another!'

Val Jeans-Jakobsson

Early years wishing well: People who help us

A good neighbour

Personal, social and emotional development

★ Encourage the children to talk about friends, family and neighbours who help them and what they do to help.

★ Discuss things that the children do to help others and how helping others makes them feel about themselves.

★ Ask the children to think of a person who may help in your setting and paint pictures for them as special way of saying 'thank you'.

★ Highlight examples of kindness in the group and thank individual children.

Communication, language and literacy

★ Invite the children to help you to create a shopping list for the greengrocer's. Provide the children with the resources to create lists of their own in role-play.

★ Play 'I'm going shopping for my neighbour to buy...' taking it in turns to repeat the list, adding a new item each time. See how many things the children can remember. If they find this difficult, have examples of a few items for them to choose from and place them from left to right as the children make up the order of their rhyme.

Mathematical development

★ Set up a shop with a small range of familiar food packaging. Make simple lists showing pictures and a number to indicate how many of each item to buy.

★ Put different quantities of raw carrots into self-seal clear bags (make small holes in the bags for safety) and order them like a number line along the floor. The children can help you to count them out.

Knowledge and understanding of the world

★ Bake some cakes decorated like those in the story.

★ Grow carrot tops by cutting the tops off carrots and placing them in a shallow dish of water, so that the children can observe the growth over a period of time.

Physical development

★ In a large group, pretend to carry an empty bag to the shop and add items of shopping, one by one. Encourage the children to change their pace as they imagine their bag becoming heavier. As the children walk home, they can pretend to knock on doors and give items to their neighbours. Their pace can become quicker again as their bags gets lighter.

Creative development

★ Make 'thank you' cards for people that the children know. Encourage them to draw pictures to illustrate what they are saying thank you for.

★ Print pictures using carrots with just the tops removed so that they are easy to hold. Help the children to mix a selection of shades of orange paint.

Geraldine and the bus drivers

Every Tuesday, Geraldine and her mum took the bus to the library in the big town. But this Tuesday, there had been a terrible storm the night before, and all the passengers on the bus were talking about it.

The bus went on its way down the road until suddenly, it screeched to a stop. Everyone lurched forward, and there were cries of dismay.

'Everyone all right?' asked Harry, the driver. He was standing up at the front of the bus, looking quite pale. 'Looks like we've got a tree down.'

The storm had blown a large oak tree right across the road, blocking it completely.

Just then, they heard another screech of brakes. A second bus had arrived, going the other way.

'Well, this is a right pickle,' said Harry. 'That's Syma's bus! She can't get by, either.'

A young lady driver waved as she climbed down from the cab of the bus.

The drivers stood together looking at the tree and shaking their heads. Passengers left the bus to come and have a look as well.

'We can't drive round it,' said Syma, poking the ground with her shoe. 'The ground's much too muddy.'

'They'll probably have to get the fire brigade out. It will be a long wait for the passengers, though,' said Harry.

'I've got an appointment at nine!' said one passenger.

'I have to catch a train at half-past!' said another.

Geraldine tugged at her mum's sleeve. 'I've got an idea,' she said.

'Not now, love,' said her mum. 'Someone's called the police on their mobile. They'll sort it out.'

Geraldine tugged at Syma's sleeve. 'I've got an idea!' she said.

Syma smiled. 'Go on, then. What is it?'

Geraldine told them.

'Brilliant!' said Syma.

'Just the ticket!' said Harry. 'Why don't you tell everyone your idea?'

Geraldine went pink and spoke up. 'I think we should ... swap buses!' she said. 'We could go into town with Syma, and Syma's passengers could go to the village with Harry.'

And that's just what they did. Passengers scrambled over and around the fallen tree. Then Harry and Syma turned their buses round and went back the way they had come. Everyone was happy.

Later, the police arrived with a tree surgeon, who cut up the fallen tree and took it away in his truck. And Geraldine had her picture in the local paper, standing with Harry and Syma, as they planted a new sapling to replace the old tree.

Kim Wilcox

Early years wishing well: People who help us

Geraldine and the bus drivers

Personal, social and emotional development

★ Line up rows of chairs to look like bus seats and pretend to go on a journey to town, taking it in turns to be the driver.

★ Discuss the importance of giving up our seats on buses and other public transport for those who need it more than us.

Communication, language and literacy

★ Gather together all kinds of used tickets, encouraging the children to bring old tickets from home. Make a zigzag book of tickets. Include a label and a simple picture showing what type of ticket it is such as a bus ticket, boat ticket, train ticket and so on.

★ Provide small pieces of paper and let the children make their own travel tickets to use in role-play.

Mathematical development

★ Count out rows of toy buses or cars.

★ Look at timetables and provide blank books for the children to practise writing numbers as they create their own timetables.

★ As a large group, sit on chairs and pretend to be passengers on a bus. Roll a dice and say the number shown to indicate how many people must get off (the children can sit on the floor as you, or a child counts them off). When the bus is empty, roll the dice again to count the children back on the bus for the return journey.

Knowledge and understanding of the world

★ Discuss traffic lights and why they are used. Ask the children to talk about traffic lights that they pass on their way home. Encourage them to think about why some places have a lot of traffic lights and other places have none.

Physical development

★ Practise cutting skills by giving each child a copy of the photocopiable sheet on page 89 and asking them to cut out the bus. Attach the wheels using split pins.

★ In a large open space, give the children the opportunity to pretend to drive buses by moving forwards and backwards, taking care not to bump into others. Encourage them to turn corners and stop when you ring a bell for a passenger to get off.

★ Make simple lacing cards in the shape of buses. Use a medium weight of card and a hole-punch to make the holes, so that threading is not too difficult. The children could use lengths of string or wool to thread around their bus.

Creative development

★ Make models of buses out of empty cereal boxes. Provide paint colours typical of the buses in your area. When the paint is dry, ask the children to paint words and numbers on their bus for the number plates and route, using fine brushes and black paint.

41

The park keeper's birthday

Sam Squirrel, the park keeper, took the big iron key and unlocked the park gate, just as Postie Mole arrived with some letters for him. A crowd of young rabbits pushed past on their way to school.

'Steady on, there!' Sam called after them.

'Morning, Sam!' said Mole. 'Here's your post. Looks like bills to me!' She went on her way, grinning.

'It's always the same,' Sam said to himself. 'No one remembers a park keeper's birthday.'

He began to sweep the paths clean, singing a little song to help him.

Sweep, sweep, sweep the paths
Make them nice and ti-dy.

Then he went to the pond to make sure that the ducks were all well.

'Morning, ducks!' said Sam.

'Quack! Morning, Sam!' said the ducks.

'Mister Sam! Mister Sam!' squeaked a voice.

Sam looked down. It was one of the young rabbits.

'Arthur's fallen in the pond!' squeaked the rabbit.

'Oh, my goodness,' muttered Sam. 'Where is he?' He imagined a little rabbit struggling for his life in the water.

'There!' Sam looked to where the rabbit was pointing. A pink fluffy teddy was lying in the reeds. Sam smiled. He stretched out his broom and pulled the teddy towards him.

'Here you are,' said Sam. 'He's a bit damp, but I think he'll be all right.'

'Thank you, Mister Sam!' said the little rabbit, and he scooted off join his friends.

'It's going to be one of those days, I think,' said Sam to himself.

And he was right.

He had to rescue Mrs Hedgehog's hat from a tree. Bill Badger needed help with a puncture in his bicycle tyre, and then a group of nannies got their baby buggies in a terrible tangle.

'Who'd be a park keeper?' muttered Sam, as he picked a sandwich wrapper from the flower bed. 'You do all these things for people, and no one remembers your birthday.' It was almost time to shut the park gates for the night. He put his tools away in the shed and made his way to the gate.

'Surprise!'

Sam couldn't believe his eyes. The gates were decorated with colourful ribbons and balloons, and a crowd of animals waved and cheered. Even the ducks were there. A big banner strung across the top of the gate said 'HAPPY BIRTHDAY SAM – OUR BEST PARK KEEPER EVER!'.

Sam blew his nose. Perhaps being a park keeper wasn't so bad after all.

Jackie Andrews

Early years wishing well: People who help us

The park keeper's birthday

Personal, social and emotional development

★ Talk with the children about taking care of their environment and the importance of not dropping litter. Explain that they should always put their rubbish in a litter bin to keep the towns and countryside clean tidy.

★ Discuss how to keep safe when visiting a park or going on an outing and the importance of not talking to strangers.

Communication, language and literacy

★ Make a class book about a local park containing pictures drawn by the children. You can add photographs if available.

★ Collect a selection of leaflets from a range of parks and places of interest for the children to look at and talk about. Invite the children to bring in details of places that they have visited and give them the opportunity to talk to the group about their visit.

Mathematical development

★ Make duck finger puppets or small illustrated cards for the children to use to sing the song 'Five Little Ducks' from *This Little Puffin...* by Elizabeth Matterson (Puffin). Encourage them to count out the ducks correctly. Provide more ducks than needed so that more able children can count out additional ducks if they wish. Help the children to take away and add ducks as they sing the song.

Knowledge and understanding of the world

★ If there is a park nearby, go on a walk there together and invite parents and carers, or even teddies, to come along as well. Take a picnic if the weather allows and pretend it is a teddy's birthday.

★ Talk about the different animals which come out in the day and at night. Make a collection of books of native wild animals and, if possible, include models of animals.

Physical development

★ Give the children the opportunity to use small sweeping brushes or dustpans and brushes to help clear up spilt sand.

★ Make picnic food using salt dough. Bake till hard and paint it appropriate colours.

Creative development

★ Create a display of children in a park. Print a grass background using strips of thick card, cut from an old box. Make sure that the children dip the thin edge of the card into the paint. Draw around children to make the figures and finish them by using a variety of collage materials. Include wildlife and playground equipment or anything that is meaningful to the children in your locality.

★ Collect leaves and stick them on to a plastic surface using PVA glue. When they are completely dry, peel off and you will have a sheet of your collection of leaves to hang up, cut out or add to a display or interest table.

We'll do it in no time

'This wallpaper is looking shabby,' said Mum, looking around the living room. 'I think it's time we decorated.'

'Oh no!' sighed Dad. 'I hate decorating. It takes ages.'

'I'll help,' said Sue.

'I'll help,' said Uncle Dave.

'I'll help,' said Grandad.

'I'll help,' said Mum. 'We'll do it in no time.'

First, they all moved the furniture out of the living room. Grandad carried the chairs, Uncle Dave and Dad carried the sofa, Sue carried the cushions and Mum carried the lamps. But Sue dropped a cushion, then Mum tripped over it and dropped a lamp, so she had to clear up the mess. It all took quite a long time but at last the room was empty, except for the table that they were going to use for pasting the wallpaper.

'Now we've got to strip the old wallpaper off the wall,' sighed Dad. 'That will take ages.'

'I'll help,' said Sue.

'I'll help,' said Uncle Dave.

'I'll help,' said Grandad.

'I'll help,' said Mum. 'We'll do it in no time.'

So Dad gave everyone a wallpaper scraper. They all scraped the wallpaper off the walls, except for Uncle Dave who accidentally scraped the paint off the door instead. It all took quite a long time but at last the walls were bare.

'Now we have to cut up the new wallpaper, paste it and put it on the wall,' sighed Dad. 'That will take ages.'

'I'll help,' said Sue.

'I'll help,' said Uncle Dave.

'I'll help,' said Grandad.

'I'll help,' said Mum. 'We'll do it in no time.'

So Sue put a roll of wallpaper on the table, Grandad unrolled it, Mum measured it, Dad cut it and Mum pasted it. But Mum measured it wrong and Dad cut it too short so they had to use another roll. Then Grandad papered the door by mistake. It all took quite a long time but at last the room was wallpapered.

'That looks good,' said Dad.

'That looks good,' said Sue.

'That looks good,' said Uncle Dave.

'That looks good,' said Grandad.

'That looks good,' said Mum. 'And we did it in no time.'

'No time at all,' agreed Dad. 'It's much quicker when you have help.'

Then they all moved the furniture back into the living room and had a nice cup of tea.

Karen King

Early years wishing well: People who help us

We'll do it in no time

Personal, social and emotional development

★ Create a role-play area containing paintbrushes, buckets, rollers and trays and encourage the children to pretend to decorate the room. If possible, let the children use real water in their buckets to paint outside walls.

Communication, language and literacy

★ Create plaques on rectangles of card to label the different areas in your setting. Help the children to think of ways to illustrate each one and, if possible, add words.

★ Make a collection of home-decorating magazines. Decide on a different room each day, such as the kitchen or bedroom, and ask the children to find something that they can cut out for it. Stick the items onto a sheet of coloured card and label them. Discuss the items as a group.

Mathematical development

★ Cut wallpaper into squares, circles, triangles and rectangles. Help the children to sort the shapes into sets and name them. Encourage them to sort sets of matching patterns and colours.

★ Cut different lengths of wallpaper and attach them to the floor with sticky tape. Ask the children to identify the longest and shortest pieces. Invite the children to walk along the lengths of paper and count how many steps long they are.

Knowledge and understanding of the world

★ Look at pictures of homes from long ago and ask the children to think about how their own homes differ from them.

★ Demonstrate bathtime from past times with a doll or real baby by using either a tin bath or baby bath, filled with some water using a jug. Talk to the children about how their bath is filled at home. (Mention safety issues about hot water.)

Physical development

★ Practise cutting skills by cutting out designs or pictures from wallpaper. Use glue spreaders to stick on to paper.

★ Lay out a long length of wallpaper on the floor and give the children a range of different types of crayons and pens to trace over the patterns accurately.

★ Ask the children to reach up tall to pretend to hang lengths of wallpaper, then wave arms from side-to-side to smooth the paper from top to bottom.

Creative development

★ Print wallpaper designs on to coloured paper using a selection of household objects such as potato mashers, yoghurt pots and cotton reels.

★ Collect paint colour charts for the children to cut out several shades of their favourite colour and arrange them from the darkest to the lightest.

The Clucks' car

The Cluck family were going on their holidays today. There was so much to do! So much to remember! Mrs Cluck finished packing a hamper of food for the journey, while Mr Cluck filled the boot with the suitcases and his golf clubs.

'Come on, children!' he called. Their three little chicks all climbed onto the back seat: Daisy, Charlie and Harry. 'Where's Maisy?' asked Mr Cluck.

'Here I am!' shouted Maisy, running along clutching her favourite teddy bear under her wing. 'I nearly forgot to remember Teddy!'

Mrs Cluck sat in the front seat and fastened her seatbelt. She had to put the hamper on the floor by her feet and it was not comfortable.

'Did you remember to lock the door, Mrs Cluck?' asked Mr Cluck as he started the engine.

'No, dear. I thought you'd check that,' replied Mrs Cluck. She could feel a headache coming on.

Mr Cluck sighed, switched off the engine and went back to check the door of the hen house. It was locked.

'Have you remembered the passports and tickets, Mr Cluck?' asked Mrs Cluck.

Mr Cluck patted his pockets and brought out the travel agent's folder with everything inside. 'Yes, dear,' he said.

Mr Cluck started the engine again. The car bumped its way down the track... but then it went slower and slower, and finally came to a halt. Mr Cluck pressed the accelerator pedal with his foot, but nothing happened.

'Oh no, we've broken down!' groaned Mrs Cluck.

'Now we can't go on holiday!' wailed the little chicks.

Just then, Mr Bushtail came past in his breakdown van.

'Do you need any help?' he asked.

'Yes, please,' said Mr Cluck. 'My car won't go.'

'Let's have a look,' said Mr Bushtail. He lifted the bonnet and had a look at the engine.

'Mmm, it doesn't look as if any petrol is getting through to the engine,' he told Mr Cluck.

'Oh dear,' said Mr Cluck, going very red, 'I forgot to get some petrol!'

'Oh, no, Dad!' groaned the little chicks. Mrs Cluck just shut her eyes.

'Well, that's soon fixed,' smiled Mr Bushtail. 'I've got a spare can in my truck you can have. You can fill it up for me when you get home.'

'That's very good of you,' said Mr Cluck as Mr Bushtail poured the petrol into the tank for him.

'Can we go on holiday now?' asked the little chicks.

'Yes, you can,' laughed Mr Bushtail. 'And don't forget to have a good time!'

Karen King

Early years wishing well: People who help us

The Clucks' car

Personal, social and emotional development

★ Create a garage role-play area using large outdoor toy cars or sit-and-ride vehicles and add an assortment of safe tools. Make a petrol pump from a large cardboard box with a short length of garden hose or a length of rope pushed into the side.

★ Invite the children to talk about a car that they have been in, what colour it was and who it belonged to.

Communication, language and literacy

★ Draw a large picture of a car and ask the children to think of words to help you label it such as wheels, roof, wing mirror and so on. Model the writing of the words that they suggest. Give the children the opportunity to draw and label their own cars.

★ Make up a story with the children by asking them to predict what would happen if a car drove over some broken glass, ran out of petrol or if the lights did not work.

Mathematical development

★ Create a graph of the colours of cars that are visible from your setting. Draw a simple car shape that can be photocopied, or cut out some car shapes from white paper. Invite the children to record the colours of the cars that they can see. Display the car shapes in columns of colour and ask the children to count how many there are in each column.

Knowledge and understanding of the world

★ Talk to the children about windscreen wipers on cars and why they are necessary on rainy days.

★ Show the children a selection of familiar tools, for example, hammer, screwdriver, tape measure and spirit level. Ask the children if they know what they are and talk about what they are used for.

Physical development

★ In a large open space, ask the children to imagine that they are driving a car carefully along the road to the seaside. Practise travelling at different speeds – sometimes fast and sometimes slow. Ask the children to come to a halt as they run out of petrol. Encourage them to pretend to pour petrol into the car from a can, then continue on their journey to the seaside.

Creative development

★ Make pattern pictures using plastic cars or trucks that the children can dip into paint, then drive them along large sheets of paper. Choose vehicles of up to four colours and place in the same colour paint, this encourages the children to match the car to the paint when they finish driving.

★ Create sounds using a 'hitting' action on tins, saucepans and trays. Make loud and quiet sounds to enable the children to imagine fixing a broken car.

Mr Owl's helpers

One morning, a group of woodland friends knocked on Mr Owl's door. They carried a bucket and various bags of tools. A window flew open and Mr Owl's angry face peered out.

'What do you want?' he called.

'Help-a-Neighbour Week, Mr Owl,' said Alice Rabbit. 'We're doing jobs, collecting for animals in need. Is there anything…?'

'No there isn't!' said Mr Owl, rudely. 'Go away!'

Mr Owl shut the window so hard, a pane of glass cracked.

'Bother!' he muttered.

He went to the sink to wash up his dishes, but when he turned on the tap it gave a little judder and no water came out.

'Blow!' said Mr Owl.

On his way to inspect the water tank, Mr Owl noticed that smoke was seeping into the living room from the chimney.

'Oh, no!' he coughed. 'The chimney's blocked again!'

He climbed up the rickety stairs to the attic, pushed up the trapdoor and shone his torch at the water tank. Thick ice coated the pipes.

Mr Owl grunted. 'Well, what's a frozen pipe on top of everything else?'

On his way down the stairs, Mr Owl's foot went straight through a rotten board.

'Ow, ow ow!' he yelled. 'My foot!'

Hobbling and hopping, Mr Owl went back to his kitchen. He took out the first-aid box, but it only held two safety pins and a tin of plasters.

'Bother!' said Mr Owl, and he wondered what to do next.

There was a ring at the door.

'Mr Owl! Mr Owl! Are you all right?' called a voice.

'No, I'm not!' shouted Mr Owl. He hobbled over to the window and looked out. It was those 'Help-a-Neighbour' woodland friends again.

'We saw your chimney smoking,' said Alice Rabbit. 'Ben here is a chimney sweep. He can help.'

'Ah… erm… all right then,' said Mr Owl, gruffly. 'You'd better come up.'

Ben Badger soon started work on the chimney. Then Daisy Squirrel, a plumber, went up to fix the water pipes. Toby Weasel got out his carpenter's tools to mend the broken stair and put a board over the cracked pane of glass. And Alice Rabbit, who was a nurse, made Mr Owl sit in a chair while she took care of his foot.

'Well,' said Alice. 'It's a good job we were here!'

Mr Owl fumbled in his pocket for some money. 'Here,' he said, tipping all his cash into the bucket. 'For the animals in need. I didn't realize I needed so much help until now! Thank you.'

Jackie Andrews

Early years wishing well: People who help us

Mr Owl's helpers

Personal, social and emotional development

★ Provide different types of plastic tools in the home area along with tea towels and empty washing-up liquid bottles. Encourage both boys and girls to act out various kinds of mending and cleaning jobs that are done around their home.

★ Discuss whether any of the children's parents and carers do any of the jobs in the story. If possible, invite them in to talk to the group and show them the tools that they use to do their job.

Communication, language and literacy

★ Use small pieces of card for the children to make their own business cards. Encourage them to illustrate and write their names and numbers on the cards. Display these on your information board.

Mathematical development

★ Create an animal number shelf by placing a row of ten furry animals on a shelf, each wearing a number badge from one to ten. Start off by counting them daily and saying how old each animal is. When the children are familiar with them, take one or more away and see if the children can say which animals and how many are missing. Place them around your room so that the children can find them and return them to the correct place on the shelf.

Knowledge and understanding of the world

★ Buy ice pops from the local supermarket and freeze them. Put them into the water tray and pretend that they are frozen pipes. Invite the children to watch and feel what happens as the ice begins to melt.

★ If you have an outdoor area at your setting, feed the birds with nuts or make bird seed cakes. Let the chidren take home the bird seed cakes to put in their gardens or hang on balconies.

★ Talk with the children about which taps have hot and cold water and discuss safety when using taps anywhere without an adult.

★ On a frosty morning, find leaves covered in frost and look at them using magnifying glasses. Bring the leaves inside and watch as the frost melts, forming water on the leaves.

Physical development

★ Give the children a bowl of water and a pourer and encourage them to pour water down plastic tubing with holes in to create the effect of burst pipes.

Creative development

★ Invite the children to use wax crayons to draw pictures of owls, then water down some paint to make a colour wash in dark blue. Ask them to paint over the top to create the night sky. Give the children yellow paper to cut out a moon to stick on to their picture when the paint is dry.

Firefighters to the rescue

Pam's mum and dad are both firefighters. They work at the same fire station, but they do not work there at the same time. Dad works with Red Watch and Mum with Green Watch. That means that one of them is always at home to look after Pam.

Fire-fighting is a very dangerous job. When there is a fire, the firefighters jump aboard their engine and race off as quickly as they can. Someone may be in a burning building and in need of their help.

The firefighters put on their helmets and special clothes as they race along the streets. The fire-engine has a blue, flashing light and a loud siren to warn traffic that they are coming, so please get out of the way!

Fires can happen at any time. If there are people trapped in a burning building, the firefighters use their long ladders to help rescue them. They also search inside the building. They have to put on breathing masks to protect them from the smoke. While some of the firefighters rescue people, others are busy trying to put out the fire with water from their fire hoses.

Firefighters also have to go to road accidents, to help people who might be trapped inside their car. They use special equipment to cut them free.

Sometimes an animal gets into difficulties and needs their help. They often have to use their ladders to rescue cats that have got stuck high in a tree. Farmers are glad of their help when a cow or horse falls into a ditch or swamp: the firefighters have special gear for lifting heavy things.

When they are not rescuing people, or putting out fires, the firefighters have to practise using their ladders and other equipment. They do this while they are waiting at the fire station. It is very important that they know exactly what to do when there is an emergency.

Firefighters are very brave people. Pam is proud of her mum and dad.

Barbara Garrad

Early years wishing well: People who help us

Firefighters to the rescue

Personal, social and emotional development

★ Explain to the children what they need to do in the case of a fire and why. Hold a fire drill from time to time so that everyone knows what to do.

★ Attach some torn pieces of red, yellow and orange tissue paper on to a doll's house or around the home area and pretend that there is a fire. Encourage the children to act out their feelings through their play.

★ Create a role-play area with fire helmets, dressing-up clothes and a fire engine made out of a large box with two chairs inside and a window and doors cut out.

Communication, language and literacy

★ Write the word 'hot' on a large sheet of red paper and 'cold' on a large sheet of blue paper. Have a brainstorm session with the children to think of words of things that are either hot or cold. Give each child a folded piece of paper and ask them to write 'hot' words in red on one side and 'cold' words in blue on the other side.

★ Give each child a copy of the photocopiable sheet on page 90. Encourage them to join the dots on the picture and then the words carefully with a pencil.

★ Ask the children to draw pictures to illustrate firefighters at an emergency. Encourage each child to tell the group the 'story' of their picture.

Mathematical development

★ Explain that 999 is the telephone number for the emergency services. Ask the children to practise writing the numeral 9. Invite them to try to write their home telephone numbers.

Knowledge and understanding of the world

★ Show the children a large candle. Invite them to predict what colours the flame will be and ask them if they think it might be blue. Light the candle with the children at a safe distance to check their answers.

★ Discuss the dangers of fire and how to keep safe in the home. Talk about matches and why children should never touch them.

★ Invite local firefighters to talk to the children and show them their equipment, explaining how and why it is used.

Physical development

★ Play 'Fast firefighters' by riding sit-and-ride vehicles quickly and carefully outside pretending to travel to an emergency, either a fire nearby or a crashed toy car.

★ Give the children the opportunity to use climbing apparatus.

Creative development

★ Create fire pictures by making handprints in red, yellow and orange.

★ Paint pictures of firefighters in their uniforms. When they are dry, cut each one out and use to make a firefighter's display.

Taking care of eyes

Peter always enjoys going to see Mrs Beech, the optician. Mum takes him every six months, just after his visit to the dentist. Mum says that it is important to take care of eyes and teeth.

While he is waiting for his turn, he likes to play at trying on some of the glasses that are on show. Perhaps this time he will be allowed to have a pair.

Mrs Beech always has a good look at Peter's eyes. She shines a torch into each one and looks carefully through a special peep-hole. She says they are very healthy, which is good news. Then she plays games with him.

The first game is called 'Find the shape'. Peter is given a card with four shapes printed on it. Mrs Beech holds up her card with just one shape on it and Peter has to point to the same shape on his own card. He is very good at this game, so Mrs Beech gives him a card with six smaller shapes on it, and they do the same again. Mrs Beech is very pleased with Peter.

The game Peter likes best is called 'Animals in the jungle'. Mrs Beech holds up a card with the outline of an animal on it. Peter has to point to the animal and say what it is. Then she holds up another card. The animal is not in the same place, and it is fainter. They carry on with this game until Peter cannot see the animal at all – it has disappeared into the jungle.

They also play a game where the page is covered with lots of coloured dots. Peter has to look at it and tell Mrs Beech if he can see a shape. Then he tells her what it is and what colour it is.

Peter is very good at all these games. Mrs Beech tells his mum that both his eyes are working properly. Sometimes Peter feels a little bit disappointed. He would like to have glasses, just like his dad!

Barbara Garrad

Taking care of eyes

Personal, social and emotional development

★ Set up a role-play optician's. Include old glasses, frames, sun-glasses and unbreakable mirrors.

★ Look at pictures of characters that wear glasses, such as Harry Potter, and famous people that the children may recognize.

★ During circle time, ask the children to close their eyes and try to imagine what it would be like if they were blind.

Communication, language and literacy

★ Write out letters in a variety of sizes, similiar to a chart in an optician's. Work in small groups and encourage the children to name the letter sounds. Give the children the opportunity to make letter charts of their own and test each other as part of their play.

★ Play a matching game using letters of the alphabet. Ask the children to find the lower and upper case letters that match and see how many pairs they can find.

Mathematical development

★ Create a 'Mr Pair' display by making a large figure that has lots of pairs of items, for example, a pair glasses, a pair of shoes, a pair of trousers, a pair of socks, a pair of gloves and a jumper with his favourite number on it... 2, of course!

★ Use a set of playing cards to match pairs of the same number and colour.

Knowledge and understanding of the world

★ Give the children a selection of magnifying glasses and ask them to carefully look at a friend's eyes.

★ Show the children some Braille and invite them to close their eyes and touch it.

★ Invite a blind person with a guide dog to to talk to the children about how they manage to do everyday things, even though they cannot see.

★ Talk about why we wear sun-glasses and why it is dangerous to look directly towards the sun.

Physical development

★ As a whole group, sing 'Heads, Shoulders, Knees and Toes' from *This Little Puffin...* compiled by Elizabeth Matterson (Puffin). Encourage the children to point to the correct parts of their body as they sing.

★ Create an obstacle course in a large open space or outdoors. Provide lots of opportunities for the children to run, crawl, pull themselves along, roll and balance.

Creative development

★ Make eyepatches from ovals of card, then colour and decorate. Use a hole-punch to make two holes in the patch and use elastic to hold it comfortably on each child.

★ Make glasses from card and stick coloured Cellophane on for lenses so that the children can see their world in many colours.

The helicopter pilot

James had always wanted to fly a helicopter. Ever since he was a little boy he had told everyone that he was going to be a helicopter pilot – and now he was!

It is very exciting to be able to fly through the air and to land in unusual places. Sometimes, James lands in a field or on the top of a mountain, a tall building or even on the deck of a ship in the middle of the ocean. Wherever he lands, he has to be very careful. It is a very skilful job being a helicopter pilot.

James and the men in his helicopter crew are very important. They have to go and help people or animals that have got into difficulties and cannot be reached easily by a rescue team on foot.

One day, they had to rescue a climber who had slipped and fallen down a steep cliff. James had to keep the helicopter hovering near to the cliff, while another man – the winchman – was lowered down on a rope until he was next to the injured climber. Then a stretcher was lowered down and the man was brought up to safety in the helicopter and flown to hospital.

Another time, James and his crew had to fly out to sea to rescue some people whose boat had overturned. They were floating in their lifejackets, hoping that someone would come and help them. It took quite a long time for the helicopter crew to spot them in the water. When they did, the winchman was lowered down so that he could attach a line to one of the people in the sea. One by one, they were winched up into the helicopter. They were all very cold and wet, so the helicopter had to fly them quickly back to dry land, where they could be looked after.

In the wintertime, when the ground is covered with snow, James and his helicopter fly over the countryside dropping food to animals that are stuck in the snow. Sometimes, in very bad weather, farms and villages are cut off and need James to bring them supplies.

James is very proud to be a helicopter pilot, because he is able to help people all year round.

Barbara Garrad

Early years wishing well: People who help us

The helicopter pilot

Personal, social and emotional development

★ Create a role-play helicopter using two chairs with a patio umbrella behind to represent the rotating blades. Attach wide ribbon or tape to each chair for a seat belt.

★ Discuss with the children their own experiences of flying. Have they ever been on holiday on an aeroplane?

Communication, language and literacy

★ Play a guessing game by showing the children a variety of pictures and asking them to guess which things might be visible from a helicopter as it flies. Include things such as the sea, rivers, large buildings, roads and tiny things such as mice or a necklace.

★ Write a large 'H' on a big sheet of paper and put it on the floor. Invite the children to go on an 'h' hunt around your room to find objects beginning with the same sound and 'land' them on your landing pad. Encourage the children to write their own words on the landing pad next to their object.

Mathematical development

★ Count backwards to imagine a space rocket blasting off. Encourage the children to write numbers backwards, too.

★ Make some very high and low mountains using wet sand and provide toy helicopters and planes for the children to fly over the landscape that you create.

Knowledge and understanding of the world

★ Collect sycamore seeds and throw them into the air to observe how they move downwards. Explain that this is how the seeds use the wind to travel so that they grow in new places.

★ Look at a weather vane to see which direction the wind is blowing. Make a record each day for a week and see if it changes.

Physical development

★ Ask the children to try to turn around slowly with their arms out straight, making sure that they are not touching anyone else. Encourage them to try turning at different heights – with their legs bent and on tiptoes – and see which height is easiest.

★ If you have a large parachute for group play at your setting, use it to play games with the whole group.

Creative development

★ Create sounds to imitate the blades spinning around on a helicopter by pouring a little rice into plastic cups with lids. The children can shake them from side to side, slowly at first, and then quicker as their helicopter takes off. Ask them to slow the sounds down again as they 'land'.

★ Make spinning circles out of thin card with a blunt pencil pushed through the centre. Colour in two primary colours and watch the colour change when the spinners spin quickly.

Eleanor's nanny

Paula is Eleanor's nanny. She has looked after Eleanor since she was six months old. Eleanor's mum and dad are very busy people, so they need Paula to help them every day except Saturday and Sunday.

Eleanor loves Paula very much and Paula loves Eleanor. Every day they have lots of fun together. Paula is very good at thinking of games for Eleanor to play. One game they both enjoy is painting. Paula spreads a plastic cloth on the table and then gets out the paper, paint and brushes. Eleanor paints pictures for her mum and dad to see when they get home from work. Sometimes Eleanor gets paint all over herself. Paula just laughs, then undresses Eleanor and puts her in the bath. Eleanor likes that because she has lots of toys to play with in the water.

On sunny days, they play in the garden. Paula helps Ellen to dig in her sandpit, or play on her swing or slide. If it is a really nice day, they go to the nearby park and play on the see-saw or climbing frame.

The days that Eleanor likes best are when Paula's friends come to the house to have a nannies' get-together. This is fun because the nannies bring the children they are looking after, and

Eleanor has new friends to play with.

On Monday, Eleanor and Paula go to Music Club. Eleanor enjoys playing on the drum and singing the songs.

On Wednesday, they go to Mothers and Toddlers. This is fun because there are bikes and go-karts to ride on.

On Friday, they go to Ducks and Ducklings at the local swimming pool. They have a lovely time and Paula is teaching Eleanor how to swim.

The weeks pass very happily. But both Eleanor and Paula enjoy the weekends. Eleanor has her mum and dad all to herself, and Paula has some peace and quiet!

Barbara Garrad

Early years wishing well: People who help us

Eleanor's nanny

Personal, social and emotional development

★ During circle time, talk about all the people who look after the children. Ask them to tell each other what they like doing best with their special person and if they play with other children, too.

★ Invite a nanny, child-minder or parent to visit and talk to the children about looking after a baby. Ask them if they could give the children the opportunity to watch a baby being bathed.

★ Put an old baby bath in the water tray and supply empty baby-bath bottles and towels to create a 'doll's bath time' area.

Communication, language and literacy

★ Cut the top off a large cardboard box and paint it to create a bath. Ask the children to bring in an item that would be used in the bathroom (all bottles should be empty!). Attach a large parcel tag to each item with sticky tape and act as a scribe to write the words on some of the items. Put all the items in the bath and give the children the opportunity to write on the rest of the labels.

★ Invite the children to make bedtime story-books for their own teddies or dolls at home. Fold three sheets of paper in half and staple along the fold. Discuss favourite stories with the children and encourage them to draw pictures and write words to make a book of their own.

Mathematical development

★ In small groups, give each child a hand towel and demonstrate how to make it into many different shapes. Start off with a rectangle, then fold it in half to create a square and fold the square in half diagonally to make a triangle. Ask the children to demonstrate their shape folding to each other and to their family.

Knowledge and understanding of the world

★ Discuss the importance of washing clothes. Let the children wash some of the dolls' clothes or unwanted baby clothes brought from home. Compare them to the dirty ones. Use a baby bubble bath which is more gentle on skin than detergent.

Physical development

★ Invite the children to hang out the toys' clothes on a washing line using pegs.

★ Encourage the children to put coats on by themselves and try fastenings, too.

Creative development

★ Create 'bubble bath' self-portraits by asking each child to paint a picture of their face. Cut out circles from bubble wrap and stick them below the faces to represent the bubbles.

★ Display a collection of bath-time objects and ask the children to make observational drawings of them.

My gran and grandpa

Today is Saturday. Dad has brought me to stay at Gran and Grandpa's until Sunday. I often do that. It's good.

Dad stays for a cup of coffee, then I kiss him goodbye.

Grandpa and I write a shopping list of things I'd like for tea. Gran drives me to the supermarket. She helps me to read the shopping list and find the food. On the way back, we stop at the library for some books.

Grandpa has cooked some of my favourites for dinner. It's stew and dumplings, then banana and custard. Afterwards, we all clear up. Gran shows me how to shake the table-cloth then fold it. I put away the clean knives and forks and spoons.

We watch some television then Gran and I go to wash the car, leaving Grandpa asleep in his armchair. We put some car shampoo in a bucket, and add lots of water. Gran washes the top of the car, then helps me wash the rest. We use the hose to rinse off all the bubbles.

Grandpa is making drinks in the kitchen. I put two tea-bags in the teapot. When the tea's ready, we have a mugful each.

Later, we walk to the park and have a game of football. Me against Gran, with Grandpa playing goalkeeper!

It's almost teatime. First, Gran shows me how to make Scotch pancakes. While they cook in the frying pan, she helps me copy out the recipe to take home tomorrow. Then we have boiled eggs, toast, Scotch pancakes, and peaches! We save three pancakes for Dad.

After tea, we play 'Snap!' Then we start a jigsaw. Grandpa puts pieces in the wrong place to tease us. We tell him off, and laugh when he pulls a funny face.

We look at the photograph album next. Gran says the photos were taken about forty years ago. There's one of my dad learning to ride his new bike. *His* mummy and daddy are *my* gran and grandpa.

At bedtime, Gran helps me to read the story-book I chose at the library. Soon I'm fast asleep.

On Sunday morning, Dad arrives to take me home. I hug Gran and Grandpa, and say 'Thank you for a lovely time'.

On the way home, Dad and I stop to buy hot pizzas for dinner. I think I'll teach him how to make Scotch pancakes this afternoon.

Susan Eames

Early years wishing well: People who help us

My gran and grandpa

Personal, social and emotional development

★ Invite grandparents to visit and join in activities with the children and share refreshments together. The grandparents could help the children to get the food ready while an adult makes the hot drinks!

Communication, language and literacy

★ Compile a group photograph album of the children's grandparents and write their first names underneath each one. Look at the album together and read the names. Note whether any of the children have the same names, or if some names are very popular.

★ Write a list of different names that the children call their grandparents, such as Gramps and Nanna.

★ Play a family guessing game by giving clues, for example, 'What do you call your mum's mummy?'. Give other clues to include the words auntie, uncle, cousin and so on as answers. Point out that families can be very different; either very small or large, so some children may not have be familiar with some of the names.

Mathematical development

★ Make family trees by counting how many people are in each child's family – include grandparents, parents and siblings. Ask each child to draw a picture of them all on a tree-shaped piece of paper. Draw around a

selection of number templates and encourage each child to find the correct number for their family. They can then cut it out and stick it on to their tree trunk.

Knowledge and understanding of the world

★ Invite grandparents to bring in special things from their childhood to show to the children and talk about their memories. They could bring in photographs of themselves as children and compare their clothes to those that children wear today.

★ Talk about where the children's grandparents live and if any of them live far away, or in another country. Discuss how the children communicate with their grandparents if they are far away and how they travel to visit them.

Physical development

★ Demonstrate how to play some old-fashioned games such as 'Hopscotch', skipping and marbles. Encourage the children to have a go themselves, including drawing out their own Hopscotch grid with chalk.

Creative development

★ Make a 'Grandparents gallery' by creating pictures using oil pastels or paints. Put frames around each one using strips of coloured paper and display them together.

★ Create mats by sewing simple lines on open-weave fabric such as Binca.

Early years wishing well: People who help us

Who took care of you?

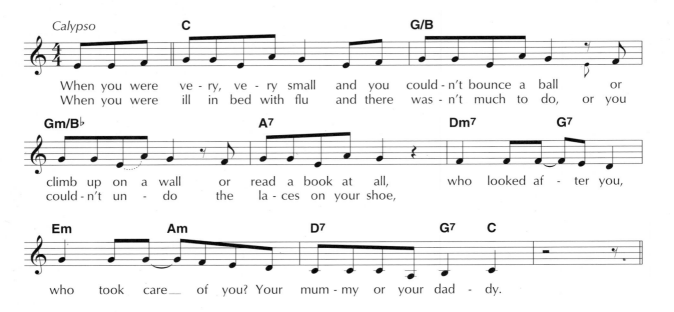

Calypso   **C**   **G/B**

When you were ve - ry, ve - ry small   and you   could - n't bounce a ball   or
When you were   ill in bed with flu   and there was - n't much to do,   or you

Gm/B♭   **A⁷**   **Dm⁷**   **G⁷**

climb up on a wall   or   read a book at   all,   who   looked af - ter you,
could - n't un - do   the   la - ces on your shoe,

Em   **Am**   **D⁷**   **G⁷**   **C**

who   took   care__   of you? Your   mum - my or your dad - dy.

David Moses

Who took care of you?

Personal, social and emotional development

★ Set up a small-world doll's house. Include children and adult dolls from a range of cultures. Set up a small-world farm using the house with examples of parent and baby animals.

Communication, language and literacy

★ Make zigzag books of 'My family', including pictures of any pets. Ask the children to write the names of everyone in their book.

★ Discuss the jobs that parents and carers do at home and act as a scribe to write down the ideas. Remember to talk about the jobs that the children help with.

★ Make a listening tape of familiar sounds of jobs around the home such as vacuuming, frying food, chopping food, washing up or running a bath. Listen with the children to see if they can identify the sounds.

Mathematical development

★ Play at sorting the family's washing out by putting a selection of adults' and children's pairs of socks in an empty washing basket. Tell the children that the washing is dry and you would like them to put the pairs together ready to put away. Include some different-sized socks of the same colour in your selection so that the children can try sorting by colour and size.

★ Lay place settings for the three bears and count how many items are needed for one bear, two bears and three bears. Ask the children how many more items they would need if Goldilocks came and how many that would be altogether.

Knowledge and understanding of the world

★ Look at pictures of parents and children from different cultures. Discuss people who live in other countries where the weather may be very different. Ask the children to share stories of visits to other countries.

Physical development

★ Play the circle game 'Here we go round the mulberry bush' and act out different jobs that parents and carers may do.

★ Give the children the opportunity to take their shoes off by themselves, then try to replace them on the correct feet and fasten them again.

★ Go on a walk with parents and carers to a local park or place of interest.

Creative development

★ Cut out some sock shapes and ask the children to paint patterns on them to create matching pairs of socks.

★ Make cards for special occasions such as 'Mother's Day' or 'Father's Day'. Let the children choose any special person that they would like to make cards for.

Friends

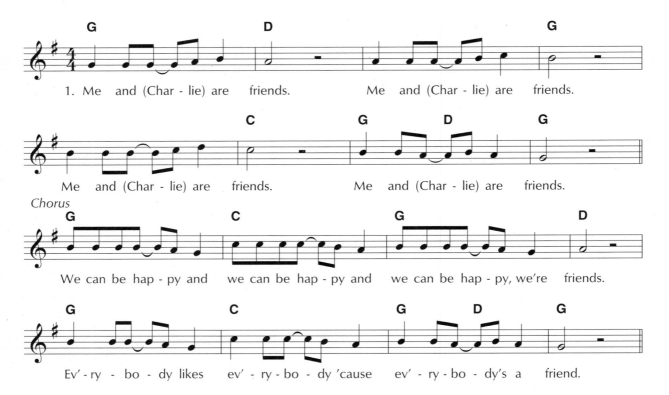

1. Me and (Char - lie) are friends. Me and (Char - lie) are friends.

Me and (Char - lie) are friends. Me and (Char - lie) are friends.

Chorus

We can be hap - py and we can be hap - py and we can be hap - py, we're friends.

Ev' - ry - bo - dy likes ev' - ry - bo - dy 'cause ev' - ry - bo - dy's a friend.

2. Me and Laura are friends (x 4)
Chorus: We can be happy...

3. Me and Jamie are friends (x 4)
Chorus: We can be happy...

> *Each verse is sung by a child (or they say the name while an adult sings) then everyone sings the chorus.*

Clive Barnwell

Early years wishing well: People who help us

Friends

Personal, social and emotional development

★ Make a 'good friends' board using a felt-covered pin board with happy pictures of children at the top. Identify the children in the group who are kind to others, write their name with a special pen on a piece of paper and let them pin it on to the board. At the end of each day, talk about all those children who have been a good friend to others. Begin each day with an empty board.

Communication, language and literacy

★ Play a listening game with everyone sitting together in a circle. Choose a volunteer and ask them to leave the circle while another child is chosen to sit under a blanket in the centre. Ask the first child to return and the one under the blanket to say 'hello'. The first child then tries to guess who it is. Give extra clues by lifting the blanket to reveal shoes and clothes or asking the child to speak again. The child under the blanket can be the next one to guess which friend is under the blanket.

Mathematical development

★ As the children arrive at the setting, ask each of them to place a cotton reel on rods that hold ten in each row. After taking the register, count out how many friends are present. Count the cotton reels one by one as a group, then count in tens any complete rows and count the extras one by one.

Knowledge and understanding of the world

★ Take photographs of each child and pin the faces onto a large map of the area. Discuss with the whole group where their friends live and demonstrate routes to a friend's house.

★ In a small group, take it in turns to use a computer to draw then print a picture for each child in the group. During circle time present each child with a picture from their friends and ask the group to think of something nice to say about each child.

Physical development

★ Hold a party at the setting. Play suitable music and invite the children to dance with their friends.

★ Ask the children to make peg pictures of their friends, by placing small pegs into pegboards to create people shapes.

★ Encourage more able children to help their friends to do up their coats, fasten their shoes and put on aprons. Show the children how to turn out the sleeves if they are inside out.

Creative development

★ Create a 'We are all friends' display by asking each child to paint a large, happy picture of their face on a circle of paper. Ask any adults to also paint their faces and display the faces together as if they were in a crowd.

★ Invite the children to beat out on a drum the number of syllables in their own name and their friends' names.

Early years wishing well: People who help us

Ask

(Tune: 'Frère Jacques')

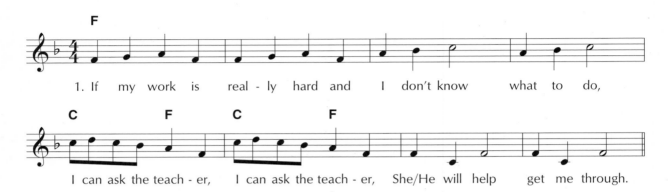

1. If my work is real-ly hard and I don't know what to do,
I can ask the teach-er, I can ask the teach-er, She/He will help get me through.

2. If I'm sick and feeling bad and
I don't know what to do,
I can ask the doctor
I can ask the doctor
He/she will help me get through.

3. If I have a tooth that hurts and
I don't know what to do,
I can ask the dentist
I can ask the dentist
He/she will help me get through.

4. If at school I spill the paint and
I don't know what to do,
I can ask the cleaner
I can ask the cleaner
He/she will help me get through.

5. If at break (play) I'm all alone and
I don't know what to do,
I can ask a classmate
I can ask a classmate
He/she will help me get through.

Hazel Priestley-Hobbs

Early years wishing well: People who help us

Personal, social and emotional development

★ Invite the children to think about and name all the people who help them, both in your setting and elsewhere.

★ Provide the children with the resources to role-play adults in your setting. Give them a register, pens, overalls, tops and anything relevant that they can use and understand. Stand back and observe the play!

Communication, language and literacy

★ Make a group address book. Use an address book or a notebook with an alphabetical index. Give each child the opportunity to find the letter that their first name begins with and write their name on that page. They can also write any letters or numbers that they know are in their address.

★ Set up a table with telephones, directories, pens and notebooks and encourage the children to think of people that they might need to telephone. Pretend that a light does not work and they need to call an electrician, or a sink is blocked and a plumber is needed. Make a list of how many people everyone can think of to call and what each person could do to help.

Mathematical development

★ Show the children a toothbrush and ask individual children to find something that is the same colour. You can extend the game further by asking for things that are longer, shorter, heavier or lighter. When the children understand the game, encourage them to play it by themselves and think up their own questions.

★ Make a 'paintbrush' number line by writing numbers on plastic cups or containers and asking the children to put the correct amount of brushes in each one, without spilling any!

Knowledge and understanding of the world

★ Discuss the clothes that are worn by doctors, dentists, cleaners and the children themselves. Look at pictures of all kinds of people who wear uniform or special clothes for work. Ask the children why they think it is important to be very clean if you work as a doctor, dentist or cook. Talk about why some work clothes usually get quite dirty, such as those of a painter, car mechanic or gardener.

Physical development

★ Pour some water onto plastic medicine spoons, without spilling any, to give to poorly dolls. Remind the children never to play with real medicine.

Creative development

★ Invite the children to paint pictures of a doctor, dentist, cleaner, painter or car mechancic, dressed in the clothes that they would wear for work.

Early years wishing well: People who help us

School cleaner

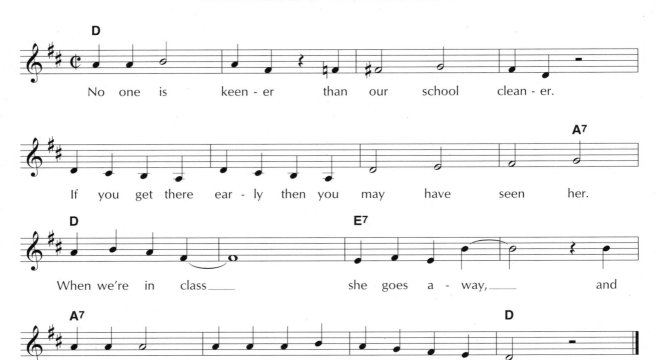

D

No one is keen - er than our school clean - er.

If you get there ear - ly then you may have seen her. **A⁷**

D When we're in class_____ **E⁷** she goes a - way,_____ and

A⁷ does - n't come back un - til we're fin - ished for the day. **D**

David Moses

Early years wishing well: **People who help us**

School cleaner

Personal, social and emotional development

★ At circle time, discuss the cleaning that takes place in your setting and who does it. If possible, introduce the cleaner to the children, so that they can learn about the cleaning chores and how they can help to look after their setting. If there are any areas that get particularly messy, the children can be encouraged to be more careful and consider the consequences of their actions on others.

★ Discuss who cleans up at home and what jobs, if any, the children help with.

Communication, language and literacy

★ Discuss all the things that the children think the cleaner would need to clean your room. Make picture zigzag books of their ideas and include words wherever possible.

★ Make 'slippery surface' signs to put up in the home area when children are pretending to clean, or near to the water tray if there is water on the floor.

Mathematical development

★ Set out a row of buckets and show a small group of 'cleaners' what they will need in order to do their job: a duster, sponge, cloth, brush and washing-up liquid. Ask the children to put one of each item into their buckets so that they all have the same. (Make sure that bottles are plastic and have been thoroughly washed out before use.)

Knowledge and understanding of the world

★ Discuss the importance of personal hygiene including flushing toilets and remembering to wash hands properly.

★ Practise washing hands properly and drying them, too. Help the children to cut out handprints and display them by toilets and sinks to help them remember to flush, then wash!

★ Go outdoors on a wet day and ask the children to walk carefully across large, white sheets of paper. Observe the dirty footprint patterns and discuss the importance of using the doormat to wipe feet and help keep the floor clean.

★ Discuss the importance of never touching cleaning products and keeping them in a safe place.

Physical development

★ Provide a selection of cloths and put a little bubble bath into the water tray so that the children can help to care for their own equipment by cleaning old toys.

★ Give the children the opportunity to use dustpans and brushes to sweep up different things such as sawdust, sand, leaves, construction bricks, corks and pebbles.

Creative development

★ Make pink and purple printing patterns using sponges, washing-up brushes, plastic pan scourers and nail brushes.

The school cook

(Tune: 'Yankee Doodle')

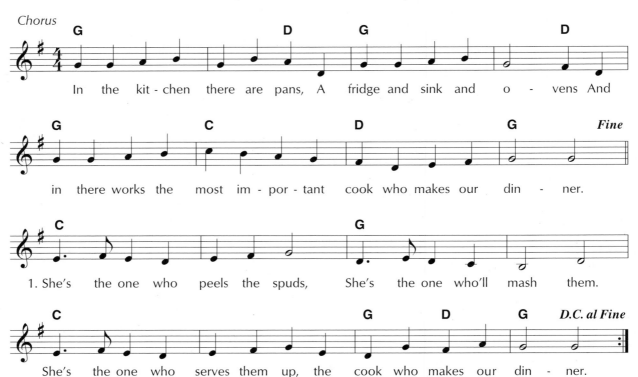

Chorus

In the kit - chen there are pans, A fridge and sink and o - vens And

in there works the most im - por - tant cook who makes our din - ner.

1. She's the one who peels the spuds, She's the one who'll mash them.

She's the one who serves them up, the cook who makes our din - ner.

Chorus
2. She's the one who cracks the eggs,
She's the one who'll whisk them
She's the one who bakes the cake
The cook who makes our dinner.

Chorus
3. She's the one who makes the dough
She's the one who'll roll it
She's the one who bakes the pie
The cook who makes our dinner.

Chorus

Hazel Priestley-Hobbs

Early years wishing well: **People who help us**

The school cook

Personal, social and emotional development

★ Talk with the children about favourite foods and their personal likes and dislikes.
★ Find out if any children have concerns about having meals away from home and try to resolve them.

Communication, language and literacy

★ Give each child a copy of the photocopiable sheet on page 91. Ask small groups of children to cut out the pictures and order them correctly from left to right. Invite the children to draw their own set of cards showing how to make a sandwich of their choice.
★ Collect a selection of take-away menus to attach to a pin board in the home area. Provide the children with paper, pens and telephones so that they can order a meal of their choice.

Mathematical development

★ Provide lots of opportunities for the children to weigh dry ingredients, such as pasta and rice, using balancing scales.
★ Give each child a circle of card to colour in to make a pizza, birthday cake or pie. Ask them to fold it in half and half again, then cut along the folds to make quarters.
★ Collect clean, empty yoghurt pots and stack them into sets. Invite the children to see which set of pots makes the highest tower.

Knowledge and understanding of the world

★ Discuss the differences in the types of food that the children eat and discuss reasons why they eat differently, for example, for religious reasons, personal choice such as vegetarians, or because of a health need for a special diet.
★ Show the children some pasta shapes and sort them into separate trays so that they can feel them. Cook the pasta and when cool let the children touch it again and ask them to describe the change in texture.

Physical development

★ Make sandwiches and practise spreading fillings. (Be aware of any food allergies and dietary requirements.) Share with the children and make a special lunch for the school cook.
★ Practise using rolling-pins and mixing ingredients to make gingerbread people.
★ Give each child a copy of the photocopiable sheet on page 92 and ask them to complete the picture using crayons or felt-tipped pens. Cut the gingerbread men out carefully and stick them on to coloured sugar paper.

Creative development

★ Create sounds with upturned saucepans, blocks of wood and metal spoons. Make shakers by putting dried pasta and pulses into plastic cups and sealing them. Find out whether you get different sounds by mixing different pulses and pastas together.

Early years wishing well: People who help us

My heavy bag

(Tune: 'Have You Seen the Muffin Man?')

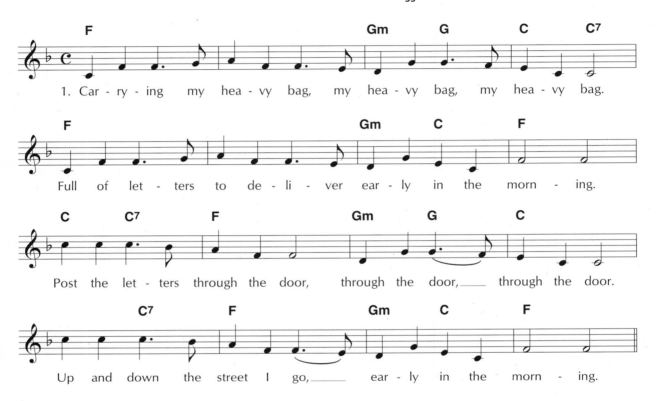

1. Car - ry - ing my hea - vy bag, my hea - vy bag, my hea - vy bag.

Full of let - ters to de - li - ver ear - ly in the morn - ing.

Post the let - ters through the door, through the door,___ through the door.

Up and down the street I go,___ ear - ly in the morn - ing.

2. There are numbers on the doors, and numbers on the envelopes.
It's my job to match them up, early in the morning.
Match the numbers carefully, carefully, carefully.
Up and down the street I go, early in the morning.

Sanchia Sewell

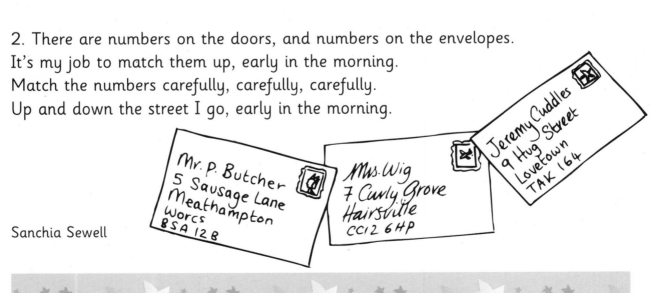

Early years wishing well: People who help us

My heavy bag

Personal, social and emotional development

★ Let the children pass an addressed parcel around a circle and talk about what they would like to be inside it and why.

Communication, language and literacy

★ Provide paper and envelopes for the children to use to write and make their own letters and cards.

★ Match the names on letters on the photocopiable sheet on page 93.

★ Act as a scribe to demonstrate writing an address, then help the children to write either numbers, names or words in their own addresses.

Mathematical development

★ Display a post bag with letters placed in it for the children to count each day, both as a group and individually. Keep a record and talk together about which day you received the most post.

★ Wrap a few items in brown paper and ask the children to guess which are the lightest and heaviest parcels.

★ Make a large parcel very light and a small one heavy, then ask the children to predict the heaviest.

★ Create a display of birthday cards that have numerals on them and create playdough cakes with birthday-cake candles to match to the cards.

★ Hang a row of houses on a washing line with numbers from 1 to 10 on the doors.

Knowledge and understanding of the world

★ Create a display of cards linked to celebrations from other cultures. Help the children to make their own cards to celebrate these occasions.

★ Collect postcards from different countries and look at a globe to see where they may be from. Ask parents and carers to send postcards to your setting when they take their children on holiday. Display these for everyone to see.

Physical development

★ Wrap junk boxes to create parcels. The children can use sticky tape and string to secure their packages.

★ Let the children experience the feeling of carefully carrying bags of different weights (nothing too heavy!). Ask them to consider why heavy things are taken in vans and not carried by a person.

Creative development

★ Provide a range of collage materials, glue and card and invite the children to create cards for any occasion.

★ Let the children create a post van for role-play. Use a very large cardboard box with the top cut off, paint it red and place a chair inside. Make a post-box out of a smaller box.

Early years wishing well: People who help us

Newspaper boys and girls

(Tune: 'Au Clair de la Lune')

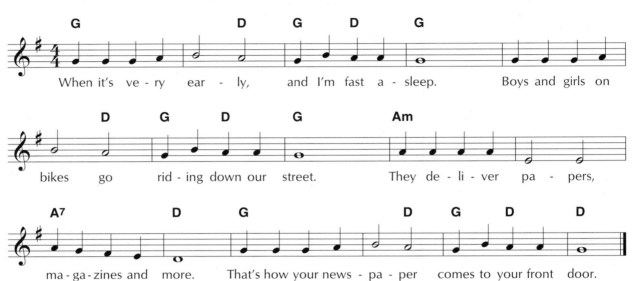

When it's ve-ry ear-ly, and I'm fast a-sleep. Boys and girls on bikes go rid-ing down our street. They de-li-ver pa-pers, ma-ga-zines and more. That's how your news-pa-per comes to your front door.

Sue Nicholls

Early years wishing well: People who help us

Newspaper boys and girls

Personal, social and emotional development

★ During circle time, ask the children to discuss whether they have any papers or comics delivered. Ask the children to bring old newspapers, comics and magazines to share or recycle. Use the newspapers to cover surfaces during art and craft. Invite the children to read or cut up the comics. Display the magazines for parents and carers to borrow or use them for cutting and sticking. If you have too many, take them to a recycling point and talk with the children about the importance of looking after the environment.

Communication, language and literacy

★ Each morning write the day and the date at the top of a large blank sheet of paper and explain that it is the front page of a newspaper. At the end of a session, act as a scribe to write news from that day and important things about your setting. At the end of the week, look back at the things that have happened.

★ Collect a selection of different newspapers and read the name of each one to the children. Ask them if they recognize any of the papers.

Mathematical development

★ Put some newspapers in bags and ask the children to hold the bags and identify which one is the heaviest and which is the lightest.

★ Give each child a copy of the photocopiable sheet on page 94. Ask the children to count the houses and write the numbers below them, then decide how many papers are delivered to each home. Place counters to represent papers and count how many are delivered altogether.

Knowledge and understanding of the world

★ If possible, show the children newspapers or magazines from other countries so that they can develop an awareness of other styles of writing and different languages.

★ Invite the children to look at newsprint with magnifying glasses.

Physical development

★ Give the children the opportunity to use different types of shape-posting toys and discuss the names of the shapes.

Creative development

★ Create black and white shape prints by printing with black paint on white paper and white paint on black.

★ Find out the children's house numbers (or ask them to choose a favourite number if they cannot remember or do not have one) and help them to make the number by sticking dried pasta on to card. You may need to help the children to draw the correct number in an appropriate size on the card before they stick the pasta on.

At the baker's

(Tune: 'She'll Be Coming Round the Mountain')

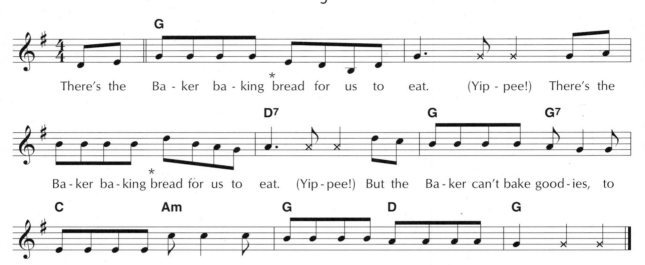

There's the Ba-ker ba-king bread for us to eat. (Yip-pee!) There's the
Ba-ker ba-king bread for us to eat. (Yip-pee!) But the Ba-ker can't bake good-ies, to
feed our hun-gry tum-mies, With-out the right in-gre-dients in the bowl. (Quite so!)

*Substitute other 'goodies' that the baker bakes. Ask the children for their ideas, then sing a new verse for each new 'goody', for example, roll or cakes.

Peter Morrell

Early years wishing well: People who help us

At the baker's

Personal, social and emotional development

★ Visit a baker's shop and look at all the different things that they sell.

★ Set up a baker's shop using play cakes and bread or make your own using baked salt dough. Provide aprons and hats, bags and a till for the children to role-play.

★ Discuss what cakes or breads the children's family members bake at home and what the children like the most.

Communication, language and literacy

★ Show the children a few cakes and then put them into a shoebox and close the lid. Give clues about a cake and ask the children to guess which one you have chosen for tea. Invite the children to peep into the box, choose a cake and then give clues.

★ Look at cookery books and find recipes and pictures of cakes. If possible, find illustrations of birthday cakes and ask the children in small groups to find their favourite.

Mathematical development

★ Make five big currant buns by decorating large sheets of card and cutting a hole near to the top of each one, big enough to fit over a child's head. Choose five children to be the cherries on the buns in the shop and sing the rhyme 'Five Currants Buns', inviting other children to buy the buns one by one.

★ Ask the children to talk about and colour

the photocopiable sheet on page 95. If possible, have real examples of different shapes of cake or use play food, so that the children can visualize the shapes more easily.

Knowledge and understanding of the world

★ Bake bread rolls with the children and let them take one home each to share with their family.

★ Ask the children and staff to each bring in a slice of bread from home and place them on a low table. Invite all the children to compare the different breads looking at colour and texture and talk about the names of any unusual types. Try to include breads from other cultures, if possible.

Physical development

★ Add bubble bath to the water tray and let the children use whisks to beat air in and create lots of bubbles.

★ Make sand pies and cakes using wet sand and a selection of bowls and moulds.

Creative development

★ Decorate white paper bags with pictures of cakes and loaves of bread. Ask the children to draw bakery food, colour it in and cut it out to make their own bag of goodies from the baker's shop.

★ Cut out circles of brown sugar paper and paint pastel colour designs on to create iced biscuits.

The shopkeeper's song

(Tune: 'Lavender's Blue')

Group 1:

Shop - keep - er   what can you sell when   we   vi - sit   you?

Shop - keep - er   what can you sell? Please give   us   a   clue.

Group 2:

1. I   can   sell   sweets, co - mics, pa - pers, ma - ga - zines   too.

That's   what   I   sell   when I get a   vi - sit from   you.   Q: Who am I?
A: Newsagent

2. Pens, pencils, crayons, paper and glue. (Stationer)
3. Chops, chickens, sausage, meat for a stew. (Butcher)
4. Leeks, cabbage, sweet potatoes and fruit. (Greengrocer)
5. Rolls, doughnuts, buns and bread fresh and new. (Baker)
6. Mice, gerbils, hamsters, bones that dogs chew. (Pet)
7. All kinds of things, I'm 'super' that's true. (Supermarket)

> *Group 1 sings the question – 'What can you sell?'*
> *Group 2 sings the clues (perhaps with actual items or drawings of*
> *them!) then asks Group 1, 'Who am I?'. Can the children suggest other*
> *shops and suitable clues?*

Peter Morrell

Early years wishing well: People who help us

The shopkeeper's song

Personal, social and emotional development

★ Create a role-play shop based on the children's first-hand experiences of local shops.

★ Encourage the children to bring along the best thing that they have bought from a shop to 'show and tell' at circle time.

Communication, language and literacy

★ Record the children singing 'The shopkeeper's song' then listen to it together and identify the names of the different shops.

★ Ask the children to describe items in a shopping bag for the others to guess.

★ Write or draw shopping lists.

★ Give the children copies of the photocopiable sheet on page 96 and ask them to draw something in the shop window to show what kind of shop it is. Let them guess what each other's shops are.

Mathematical development

★ Price items in a role-play shop up to 5p and provide real one pence pieces in play money for the children to count out. Join in with their play to develop counting skills.

★ Sort everything in the shop into sets of things that cost the same amount. Count the items in each set.

★ Make toast using square slices of bread. Cut it into two rectangles, then four squares, then triangles, then eat them up!

★ Look at the children's shoes to see what size they take. Sort a selection of shoes by size, starting with the smallest.

Knowledge and understanding of the world

★ Take small groups to visit a local shop of your choice and make a purchase. Show the children the range of items that they can buy.

★ Invite the children to share their knowledge of the locality by creating a map of nearby shops.

★ Use a variety of vegetables to make a soup. Give the children the opportunity to help chop, with plenty of adult support. Observe the difference between the raw and cooked vegetables.

Physical development

★ Practise cutting and spreading skills by using old magazines to provide lots if items to cut and stick. Create a collage of things in a particular type of shop.

★ Stack empty drink cans or food packets accurately to create a display.

Creative development

★ Paint pictures of different fruit at a greengrocer's, using real fruit as a stimulus. Look at pictures of still-life fruit paintings.

★ Give each child a copy of the photocopiable sheet on page 96. Ask them to turn it into a shop of their choice. Make a high street display with a row of different shops.

The lorry driver

1. The wheels go round and round and round, the lor-ry dri-ver's come to town, and

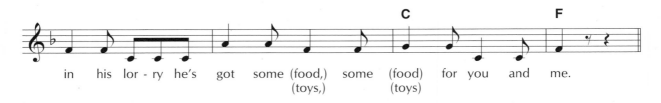

in his lor-ry he's got some (food,) some (food) for you and me.
(toys,) (toys)

Clive Barnwell

Early years wishing well: People who help us

The lorry driver

Personal, social and emotional development

★ Create lorries with the children by attaching empty cardboard boxes to the back of tricycles. Provide lots of smaller, empty boxes and plastic containers so that the children can load up their lorries.

Communication, language and literacy

★ Make a word 'Snap!' game with vehicle words such as lorry, truck, car, motorbike and so on. Include pictures if the children need an easier version. Draw and write out the set, then photocopy on to card and cut the individual cards out.

★ Look at pictures of road signs and discuss what they tell us. Ask the children to guess what some may mean. Look at other signs around you, including emergency exits.

Mathematical development

★ Load lorries with coloured bricks or counters by rolling a colour dice, then loading it up with something of the same colour.

★ Load toy trucks and lorries with bricks of different sizes and count how many each can hold. Compare how many bricks of different sizes will fit in each lorry.

★ Collect some unwanted keys and sort them by length starting with the longest key.

★ Thread beads in traffic light colours, red, orange and green then repeat this pattern to the top of the lace.

Knowledge and understanding of the world

★ Mix icing sugar with a little water and attach red, orange and green sweets onto chocolate wafer biscuits to create traffic lights. (Be aware of any food allergies and dietary requirements.)

★ Discuss metal and shiny paint surfaces on lorries and how reflections can be seen in them. Ask the children to look around the room to find shiny surfaces and look at their own reflection.

★ Roll toy lorries along different-textured surfaces and compare how easily and quickly they move along.

Physical development

★ Load small toy lorries and trucks with construction game pieces, so that they do not fall off when moving.

Creative development

★ Make 'wheel-track patterns' using toy vehicles and traffic-light coloured paints.

★ Create a 'silver and shiny' collage using metallic paper, foil, milk-bottle tops, sequins, and shiny buttons and stick on to round sheets of black sugar paper.

★ Cut out card lorry stencil shapes and invite the children to place them on to white paper, then splatter runny paint from brushes on to the paper. Lift the stencil carefully, leaving the white lorry shape. (Remind the children not to move the stencil as they work.)

79

Pet match

cat

dog

mouse

rabbit

Lollipop, 'Stop!'

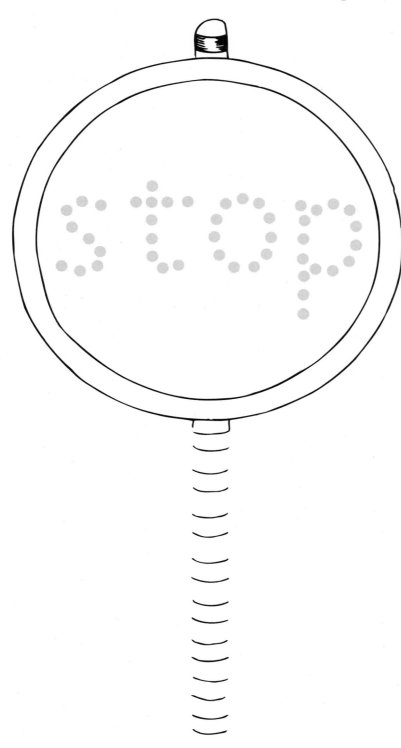

Serve it up!

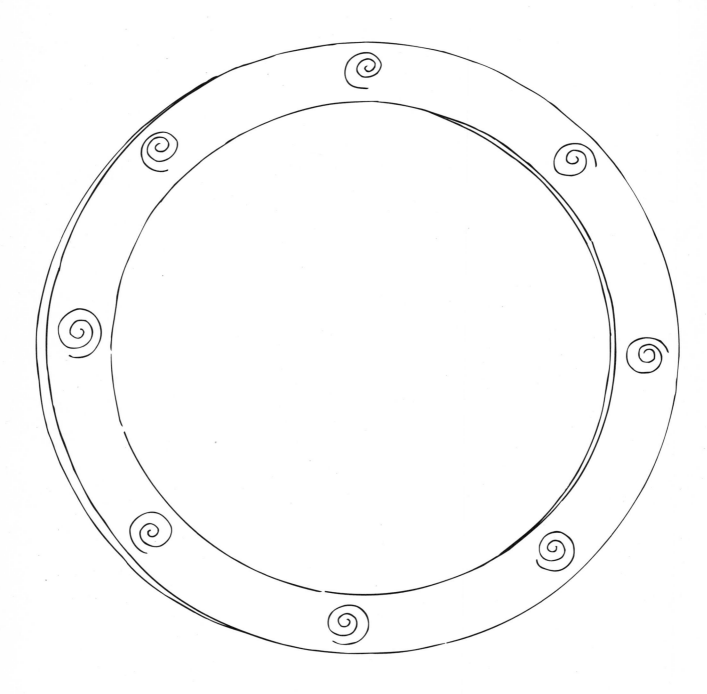

Houses in a row

Police dot-to-dot

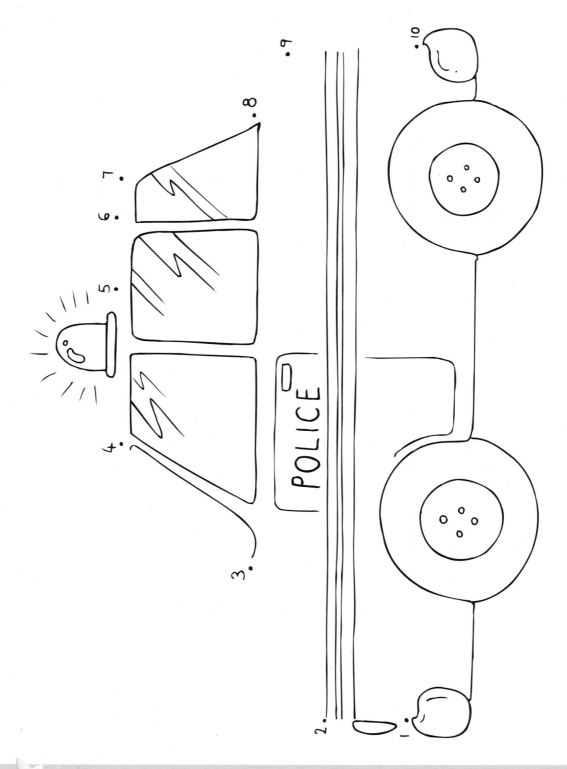

What do you do? (1)

school cook

milkman

policeman

baker

What do you do? (2)

doctor

dinner lady

car mechanic

firefighter

What's missing?

Hair flair!

The wheels on the bus

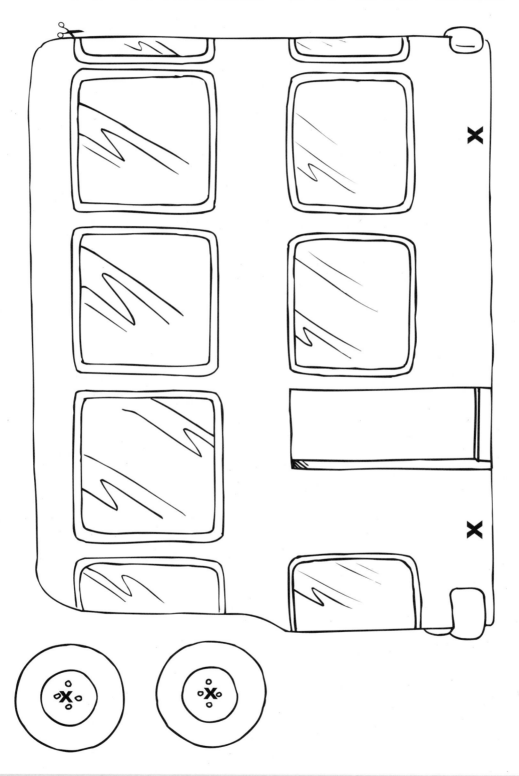

Firefighter fun

friendly firefighter

■SCHOLASTIC

Make a sandwich

Gingerbread decoration

Send a letter

Jennie .

Nigel .

Sue .

Harrison .

Natalie .

Nigel

Sue

Natalie

Jennie

Harrison

SCHOLASTIC

Down the road

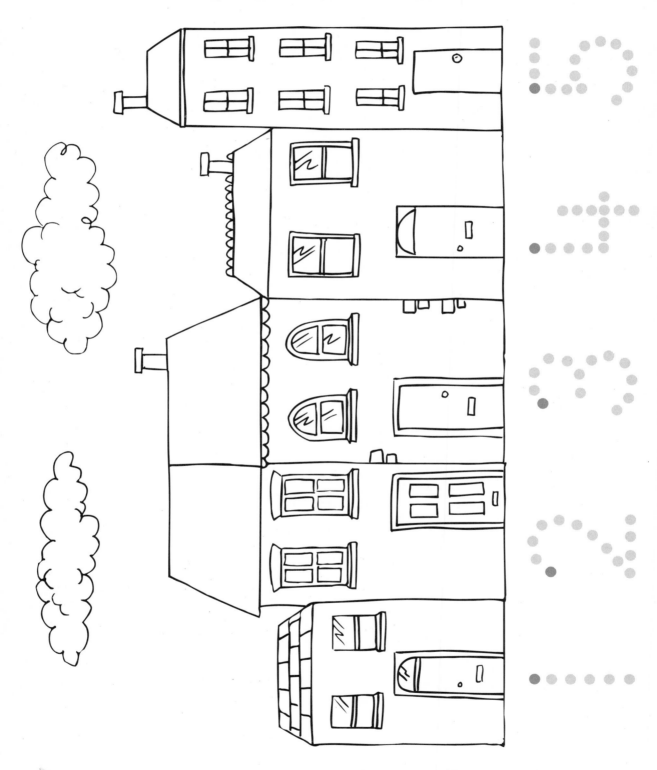

Early years wishing well: People who help us

All kinds of cake

Shop front